HOW TO WRITE A WINNING C.V.

HOW TO WRITE A WINNING C.V.

A Simple Step-by-Step Guide to Creating the Perfect C.V.

ALAN JONES

ARROW
BUSINESS BOOKS

Arrow Books Limited 1996

1 3 5 7 9 10 8 6 4 2

© Alan Jones 1990, 1996

First published by Century in 1990
This edition published by Arrow Books Limited
20, Vauxhall Bridge Road, London, SW1V 2SA

Random House Australia (Pty) Limited
20 Alfred Street, Milsons Point, Sydney
New South Wales 2061, Australia

Random House New Zealand Limited
18, Poland Road, Glenfield
Auckland 10, New Zealand

Random House South Africa (Pty) Limited
PO Box 337, Bergvlei, South Africa

Random House UK Limited Reg. No. 954009

Papers used by Random House UK Ltd are natural, recyclable
products made from wood grown in sustainable forests. The
manufacturing processes conform to the environmental regulations
of the country of origin.

Printed and bound in Great Britain by The Guernsey Press Co., Ltd

Random House UK Ltd Limited Reg. No. 954009

ISBN 0 09 972891 5

Companies, institutions and other organizations wishing to make
bulk purchases of any business books published by Random House
should contact their local bookstore or Random House direct:
Special Sales Director
Random House, 20 Vauxhall Bridge Road, London SW1V 2SA
Tel: 0171 973 9670 Fax: 0171 828 6681

Acknowledgments

Special thanks to Judith Brown, Mike Potter and John Whapham for their professional advice, and also to Eric Adams for his immeasurable support. Thanks also to all those who gave permission for their CVs to be used as case studies.

Contents

Contents

Introduction

Job hunting is a serious business, but if it were a game it might be described as follows:

'This is a game for any number of players. The game is divided into two halves: the first half is called "Application", the second half is called "Interview". All players will begin the first half but not all will be playing in the second half. The object of the game is to achieve the job offer and there can only be one winner. In the first half of the game, each player must overcome certain hazards designed to prevent him or her from qualifying for the second half. Typical Application hazards are "too old", "lacks experience", "job hopper" and "not qualified". Players who successfully negotiate these hazards are declared winners and will go on to play "Interview". Further hazards are encountered at "Interview", including "no confidence", "talks too much", "shifty", "untidy" etc. At the conclusion of the game the player who has overcome all of the hazards is declared the winner and receives the job offer. All remaining players, who had previously been winners, are now losers.'

Now, what makes this game particularly interesting is that few players can play both halves of the game equally well. One player may be a star turn when playing Application but a consummate duffer at Interview. Conversely, another player might play an excellent game of Interview but won't get the chance to prove it until the Application hazards can be overcome.

But what is it that separates the winners from the losers? The eventual winner of the game is not necessarily the best person for the job. Indeed, the best person for the job is frequently eliminated in the first half. No, the winner of the game will always be *the player who has played the game the best*. This fact alone goes quite some way towards explaining why perfectly sound job applicants find job offers, or even interviews, difficult to come by. Knowing how to play the game is the key to success.

As with all games there are rules. This book will teach you the rules as they apply to the first half of the game. It is a book for all players: for school-leavers seeking their first job and for management-level players who are moving from one job to another.

Before we play the game, a word about luck. Chance can be an important element of some games and job hunting is no different. Even a winning CV cannot be a winner for all games and you would certainly be fortunate if you got to the interview stage on every occasion. Job hunting can be exhilarating, challenging and rewarding. It can also be worrying, frustrating and a chore. What *is* certain is that many players trust too much to luck, perhaps because it is a pleasant substitute for hard work. Constructing a winning CV is not easy – but then, as the well-known maxim goes, if something is easy it is generally not worth doing. Whoever said, 'It's funny, the harder I work the luckier I seem to get', was probably a very good player.

1 Application

WHAT IS A 'WINNING CV'?

How often have you heard someone say 'I am applying for a job'? We tend to say it as a matter of course and without thinking about what we really mean. But it is arguably the most misleading statement to be found in the job-search game. It is certainly true that the overall objective is to achieve the job offer, but we know that no one gets a job offer without at least a cursory interview. The reason for playing the game of Application is to secure, not the job offer itself, but entry to the quite different game of Interview. You are, then, applying not for the job but for the *interview*.

No CV ever got anyone a job *directly*. Once the interview is secured the game of Application is over; the CV has fulfilled its role and, although it has a further role to play at Interview, its task is all but completed. All of this has an important bearing upon the content, style, format and length of the CV. The game of Application is a *damage limitation exercise*. You would be very fortunate indeed to reach the end of the game completely unscathed – there are too many hazards flying around for that to happen.

A winning CV is a *relevant* CV. It is not practicable, nor is it necessary, to compose a CV for every job application. We will be looking at CVs which could reasonably be used for most of the jobs for which you will be applying, because in practice few job hunters seriously apply for positions covering a vast range of expertise and functions. The more irrelevancies you have on your CV the less likely you are to get an interview. The inclusion of such irrelevancies can also be an indication that you are targeting the wrong jobs.

A winning CV is one which is likely to *secure the greatest number of job interviews*. The role of those responsible for recruitment and selection is not an enviable one: selecting the right person for a job is not an exact science and, being only human, recruiters' subjective instincts can take precedence over objective ones, particularly if they have not been properly trained. Many job applicants have been offered positions because of the way they look rather than any objective analysis of their ability to do the job. Fortunately this particular hazard does not arise during the game of Application, yet it is certainly true that applicants are sometimes denied interviews on the basis of where they went to school, their outside interests and the colour of the paper used for their CV. Many (though not all) of these 'irrational' hazards can be overcome, and one hazard on its own may not be harmful enough to prevent you from getting an interview. The recruiter's decision should be based upon the combined effect of all elements of your CV, some of which will weigh more heavily than others. In effect, what you include on your CV will give the reader a *mental picture of who you are*, and even what they think you might look like.

The good news is that it is *you* who decide what will go on your CV and the emphasis it will be given. It is you who bring together the elements that make up the picture, which the reader will then interpret. Problems arise when you send wrong signals. Signals to avoid are those which might provoke the reader to say 'irrelevant experience', 'too young/old', 'too negative' or any one of a number of signals which invite the response 'No'. You need to send signals which say 'confident', 'enthusiastic', 'an achiever', 'adaptable' – signals likely to encourage the reader to say 'I must see this person *to find out more*'.

A winning CV must make the recruiter's job as easy as possible. During Application those finally selected for interview will be those who have given clear, concise information, and *evidence*, to convince the reader that they are worth seeing. Evidence can cover a number of areas such as skills, experience, qualifications and achievements. If insufficient evidence is pre-

2

sented, recruiters will be unable to justify to themselves, or to their superiors, the arrangement of an interview.

Applying for interviews is a *selling* exercise. Not many of us are good at selling anything, least of all ourselves. Even when we understand the need for it there seems to be an inbuilt reluctance to 'blow our own trumpets'. This is a grave error and inability/reluctance to sell the 'product' (ie yourself) can very quickly be identified on CVs which comprise little more than a list of previous employers and responsibilities, supported by irrelevant and negative information. The problem this presents to the reader, which is ultimately *your* problem, is that there is no way of knowing if you are simply being modest or whether you have a lot to be modest about.

As consumers it is the packaging of a product, rather than the product itself, which first attracts us. The packaging or sales literature should provoke our interest enough to make us open the box, see the product and test whether it can:

1. Do what the packaging says it can do.
2. Fulfil the needs that we, the end user, have.

The analogy is a very real one, and not intended to be degrading or impersonal. You are the product, your CV is your packaging and the employer is the consumer. A winning CV must be *stimulating* enough to generate the interest of the reader.

Perhaps the greatest benefit of constructing a winning CV is that you are clearly and concisely setting the agenda for the interview. It is a compilation of all the things that *you* want to discuss, so obviously then you must *know* your CV. If you have designed it to provoke questions, which you should have, then make sure you have some idea of the types of question you want to provoke. For this reason you must have enough confidence in your CV to be able to back it up at a meeting. A winning CV may get you an interview, but if you cannot support it the end user will see it as no more than 'hype'.

For this reason a winning CV must be *truthful*. If you fall into the trap of telling lies (eg, claiming qualifications/experience you do not possess), you will be fooling no one but yourself. You will be cheating at the game, will not be able to back up your assertions at the interview, and will ultimately fail.

3

Obviously you want to minimize the risk of not getting an interview, but this is done by *leaving out* certain things, not by *putting in* half-truths or untruths: the greatest sin you should be guilty of is the sin of omission. It is not your responsibility to tell the consumer what the product *can't* do. After all, an advertisement which stated that 'this car cannot travel from 0–60 mph in less than ten seconds' would be unlikely to take your breath away.

Chief characteristics of a winning CV

A winning CV:

- Is brief
- Is relevant
- Sends the right 'signals'
- Provides evidence
- Is a selling document
- Is stimulating and provocative
- Inspires confidence
- Is truthful
- Is an agenda for the interview.

WHAT ARE YOU SELLING?

Above all else, your CV must sell the *skills* which allow you to do the job. Regardless of what we are, whether school-leavers or senior managers, employers expect us to *get results*: that is why we are paid. Skills allow us to get results, and you can identify the skills you have by analysing the type of results you have achieved in the past. Remember that you may well have the skills to do the job *even if you have no direct experience* in the type of job you are seeking: showing that you possess the skills can compensate for lack of experience.

You may have *transferable* skills. For example, if you are seeking your first management position you may already pos-

4

sess a management skill or skills without realizing it. A manager is by definition a leader: you may have developed leadership skills outside the working environment, eg, within school or social activities. A manager must have good communication skills: if you have developed your verbal and written skills then, provided you can supply the evidence to back it up, say so on your CV. A manager must be a good organizer: do you have organizational skills? If so, say so.

The great advantage with selling skills is that the arena within which the skill has been learnt and developed is not always of paramount importance – the important factor is that you have it. You may be short on direct experience and you may have no qualifications to sell, but you must have skills either of a practical nature or arising from your character and personality. All jobs require what are called 'interpersonal skills', ie a capacity to relate to and communicate with others. Some jobs rely heavily on these skills, eg, jobs requiring you to deal with members of the public. These skills can be identified as verbal or written and, again, may not necessarily have been developed through work experience.

It is one thing to identify skills but quite another to describe them in the most appropriate and telling way. The following 'Skills description words' will be useful when highlighting your skills on the CV. Completing the Skills analysis exercise on pages 12–19 will greatly enhance the quality of your CV.

Skills description words

Addressing	Forecasting	Producing
Administering	Founding	Promoting
Advising	Generating	Proposing
Analysing	Guiding	Providing
Approving	Heading	Recommending
Arranging	Identifying	Recruiting
Assessing	Illustrating	Redesigning
Broadening	Implementing	Reducing
Budgeting	Improving	Refining
Classifying	Increasing	Reorganizing

Coaching
Collating
Combining
Composing
Conceiving
Conducting
Consolidating
Controlling
Converting
Co-ordinating
Counselling
Creating
Cutting
Decreasing
Defining
Delivering
Demonstrating
Designing
Despatching
Developing
Devising
Directing
Distributing
Doubling
Editing
Eliminating
Encouraging
Establishing
Evaluating
Expanding

Initiating
Innovating
Instituting
Instructing
Interpreting
Interviewing
Introducing
Inventing
Investigating
Itemizing
Launching
Leading
Liaising
Managing
Marketing
Mediating
Minimizing
Modernizing
Motivating
Opening
Operating
Ordering
Organizing
Originating
Performing
Pioneering
Planning
Preparing
Presenting
Processing

Representing
Researching
Resolving
Restructuring
Reviewing
Revising
Saving
Scheduling
Selling
Servicing
Serving
Simplifying
Solving
Starting
Streamlining
Strengthening
Supervising
Teaching
Testing
Tracing
Training
Transferring
Transforming
Translating
Trimming
Uncovering
Unifying
Verifying
Vetting
Widening

Experience or achievements

Experience can be defined as 'what you have done', and it can help you to identify your skills – after all, our skills develop out of the experiences we have. Experience *in itself* is often much over-rated by employers and job-seekers alike: it cannot tell an employer *how good you are* at what you have done. It is

6

important to distinguish between experience and *achievements* which, like skills, arise from experiences you have had.

A losing CV is one which 'undersells' you. This most commonly happens when applicants simply list their past employers and give job titles followed by responsibilities *and no more*. For example:

Losing CV

'Department Manager responsible for the planning and phased introduction of computer technology.'

Winning CV

'*Department Manager*. Costing, planning and phasing in of computer hardware/software – completed ahead of schedule and 10% under budget; now running at 20% cost savings per annum.'

The losing CV merely lists the 'experience'. The winning CV emphasizes the *achievement*, ie how *well* it was done. This is an example of the 'trumpet blowing' which, though hard to do, is nevertheless essential: remember that your competitors in the game may have fewer reservations about 'selling the product' than you. The winning CV not only states the achievement but *quantifies* it. Whenever you can, give evidence by quantifying in terms of 'how big?' 'how much?' 'how long?' and 'how many?'.

Private sector businesses exist for one reason – to make a profit. Even public sector employers have to keep within budgets. Employers do not employ people to give them a career, job satisfaction or salary – those are *your* needs, which during Application are largely irrelevant to the employer. The winning CV shows an awareness of this by emphasizing the fact that 'I carried out that task (experience) so well that I saved my employer *money*' (achievement). If in the past you have suggested or introduced changes which improved efficiency or

7

effectiveness then say so. If you omit to say so the employer will have little reason to see you and discuss it. It is not always easy to quantify these things but if you can, do it – it shows that you are *profit-conscious*. The employer will rightly deduce that if you have what it takes to save money in one area of activity you can probably achieve it in another – useful if you are short on direct experience in the type of job they want you to do.

To do all this successfully you have to 'bite the bullet' and be very objective about your experiences. Do not be blasé about them – this is the trap many of us tend to fall into. We spend little or none of our working time analysing our achievements; if we know our job we just get on with it and see no reason to wax lyrical about how good we are – 'It's my job and that's what I'm paid for'. Look closely at the type of job you are seeking: what skills, experience and achievements will the successful applicant be likely to have? How many of them can you provide? Put this on your CV.

Qualifications

Educational qualifications can work for you or against you. (The hazards of being over-qualified and under-qualified are discussed in Part 2.) On balance it is certainly better to have some qualifications than none at all. For certain jobs specific qualifications are essential and there is little point in applying if you do not possess them. If the job vacancy is advertised, the desirability of qualifications will be stated, but take notice of *how* it is stated. 'A degree would be desirable' indicates that non-graduates will be considered if they have other things to sell which might be of interest. 'Preferably two A levels' need not rule you out if you don't have any. However, if the words 'must' or 'essential' are used then don't waste your time or theirs by applying if you haven't got what is asked for.

Some employers are uncertain about what qualifications to ask for, and accordingly go 'over the top', perhaps because they are anxious not to have hundreds of applicants. 'Educated to degree level' is ambiguous and is simply a way of saying 'We want someone intelligent'. If you consider yourself intelligent, apply.

Older applicants can get unduly worried about their lack of qualifications. This often arises when they find themselves competing in the wrong market ie, applying to employers who traditionally recruit school-leavers or graduates. The older you get the less important educational qualifications tend to be. Anyone in their fifties is, unless they have a rare skill, unlikely to get a job with the large, well-established companies which mainly recruit from the under–45s. A small to medium sized company, however, is less likely to take risks in employing inexperienced people, however well-qualified they might be. Such a company is much more interested in skills, experience and achievements. For them to take on a school-leaver or graduate might be too risky – here today and gone tomorrow. In short, if they want to go places then they need experienced people to take them there. There are few 'job hoppers' over the age of fifty.

None of the above should be seen as a 'golden rule'. They are generalizations designed to reinforce the fact that identifying what you are selling is only half the battle – you must *sell it to the right market*. Competing in the wrong market place is a recipe for frustration and an unnecessarily protracted job-search campaign.

Loyalty

From an employer's point of view, loyalty has never been high on the list of assets an employee can bring to an organization. Employers simply want to keep good people because good people get results. Good employees are offered improved pay and conditions and promotion, not as a reward for loyalty but to encourage them to stay and continue the good work. So loyalty is rather an anachronism in the context of employment.

Employees often profess loyalty when what they really mean is commitment, hard work, pride and dedication. Over the past twenty years particularly, countless thousands of good 'loyal' employees have had their loyalty severely shaken by the realization that, when it comes to the bottom line (profit) an organization will shed people if the need for their jobs no longer exists.

Loyalty is often a comfortable excuse for career inertia. The idea that one can, or even should, stay with the same organization for the whole of one's working life ('womb to tomb') is now out-dated. Careers are increasingly being seen as something the employee must control and manage – the employer is simply the custodian for a certain period of time.

This does not mean that you should not have a 'good feeling' towards your employer. It simply means that the word 'loyalty' has no place during either Application or Interview. Older job hunters who have been accustomed to placing a high value on 'loyalty' might be tempted to stress this on their CV or application letter – resist the temptation. Unpalatable as it may sound, selling 'loyalty' is naive and will most likely give the impression that you are old, old-fashioned, or both.

Personality/character

Even if you have all of the skills, experience and qualifications required you will not get a job offer if the employer doesn't like you. Selling your personality and character is an essential part of the job hunting game, but one rarely discussed because:

1 There is a reluctance among 'professionals' to admit that selection is made on such a subjective, 'unscientific' basis.
2 Either you have an attractive personality or you have not. If not there is little you can do about it.

But is this really one part of the game which must be left to chance? Not entirely. Selling your 'social skills' is certainly an extremely important part of the interview process yet has little to do with your ability to do the job (unless such skills are an integral part of that job). During Application there is a limit to how much you can *display* personality/character attributes, apart from actually saying that you possess them. The opportunity for you to present them with *evidence* is severely restricted, but *clues* to our personality can be identified through an analysis of what we say/do (Interview) and what we *write* during Application.

For example, consider the following statements which many applicants use in a speculative letter:

> 'I will phone next Wednesday to arrange a mutually convenient time for us to meet.'

Now of course some potential employers might react favourably to such a statement. It could be interpreted that the writer is positive, confident, forceful and a 'doer'. But on the whole employers do not take kindly to receiving threatening letters and they might perceive the writer as having an arrogant and bullying personality. If you *are* going to follow up the letter (which you should if you don't hear from them within a reasonable time) then there seems little point in threatening to do so.

> 'Your expansion plans as outlined in *Business Weekly* will require the right quality of staff, with good experience and the right background . . .'

Perceptive or patronizing? The interpretation is in the mind of the reader: ask yourself how *you* would feel if you received such a letter. Because employers differ, one applicant's personality attribute can be another applicant's personality *defect*:

> 'I am very hard working, loyal and enthusiastic . . . My employer has always found me trustworthy, honest and reliable . . .'

This might not seem so bad coming from a very young and inexperienced applicant – the writer could be deemed to have a pleasant personality. But it was actually written by an experienced general manager who had been with the same company for twenty-five years. The content of the letter does not 'square' with the 'personality type' the employer is likely to be seeking. It is symptomatic of a *weak* personality – at that level it should go without saying that the applicant has all of those attributes. It is not that they are irrelevant, but the writer should really be selling other things.

11

There are few opportunities to sell personality attributes on a CV or in a letter, but the likelihood of your inadvertently selling personality *defects* is quite high if you omit to have regard for the effect your written work might have in terms of the reader's interpretation of it.

SKILLS ANALYSIS EXERCISE

The exercise on the following pages will help you to identify what you are selling. It will also help you to describe it in the most telling and effective way. The key to success lies in your ability to fashion the skill statement which most accurately describes what you want to say. Effective skill statements have two elements: skill and experience. Examples of each are as follows:

Skill	*Experience*
Advising	sales reps on quotas/targets
Demonstrating	new products to retailers
Distributing	sales literature to customers

More effective skill statements have three elements: skill, experience and achievement. For example:

Skill	*Experience*	*Achievement*
Motivating	UK sales force	to increase sales

Even more effective skill statements consist of the three elements plus *quantification* of achievement. For example:

Skill	*Experience*	*Achievement/quantification*
Motivating	UK sales force	to increase sales by 30% pa.

The *very* best skill statements consist of three elements plus quantification and *intrigue*. For example:

Skill	*Intrigue*	*Experience*	*Achievement/quantification*
Devising	unique	incentive scheme	increasing profits by £100,000 in first year

Application

An effective skill statement often has to be refined from a rather vague description of an experience. A lorry driver might say 'I just drive lorries'. Closer questioning could reveal that he:

- is a Class 3 HGV driver with an accident free record
- drives 40,000 miles per year
- delivers safely delicate equipment valued at £400,000 per load
- plans cost-effective routes
- deals with complex cross-border documentation
- carries out routine maintenance
- has established an excellent relationship with customers.

These are all things a prospective employer *needs* and *wants* to know. You must analyse your job in exactly the same way. Each of the following skill statement development exercises is headed by a vague description of an experience eg 'Talked to'. In the left hand column Who/what? write down *who* you talk to during the course of your work. Write this down next to the Skill description word in the centre column which describes most accurately the function you are performing. In the right hand column To achieve what? write down what you achieved as a result. For example:

Talked to

Who/what?	Skill description	To achieve what?
SALES REPS	Advising	ON RESULTS OF MARKET
	Addressing	RESEARCH
	Controlling	
CUSTOMERS / RETAILERS	Demonstrating	NEW PRODUCTS
	Directing	
	Guiding	
	Instructing	
PUBLIC	Inteviewing	To IDENTIFY CONSUMER
	Leading	NEEDS
	Liaising	

In the above example the following skill statements can be fashioned:

- Advising sales force on market research analysis
- Demonstrating new products to consumers/retailers
- Interviewing the public to identify consumer needs

13

Now, using this technique go through each exercise and fashion *as many skill statements as you can*. Don't worry about repetition: some skills will overlap with others but elimination and fine tuning can come later.

Carry out the same exercise to identify *transferable* skills.

| | Talked to | |
| Who/what? | Skill description | To achieve what? |

Addressing
Advising
Controlling
Co-ordinating
Counselling
Demonstrating
Directing
Encouraging
Guiding
Instructing
Interviewing
Leading
Liaising
Marketing
Mediating
Motivating
Negotiating
Ordering
Performing
Presenting
Promoting
Proposing
Providing
Recommending
Recruiting
Representing
Resolving
Selling
Teaching
Training
Translating

	Found out	
Who/what?	*Skill description*	*To achieve what?*
	Analysing	
	Assessing	
	Classifying	
	Collating	
	Defining	
	Designing	
	Devising	
	Establishing	
	Evaluating	
	Forecasting	
	Identifying	
	Interpreting	
	Interviewing	
	Investigating	
	Researching	
	Testing	
	Tracing	
	Verifying	

	Sorted out	
Who/what?	*Skill description*	*To achieve what?*
	Analysing	
	Arranging	
	Assessing	
	Budgeting	
	Classifying	
	Collating	
	Composing	
	Conceiving	
	Conducting	
	Controlling	
	Co-ordinating	
	Decreasing	
	Defining	
	Distributing	

Editing
Eliminating
Establishing
Evaluating
Identifying
Improving
Investigating
Itemizing
Modernizing
Operating
Organizing
Planning
Preparing
Processing
Producing
Redesigning
Reducing
Refining
Reorganizing
Researching
Resolving
Reviewing
Revising
Scheduling
Simplifying
Solving
Streamlining
Transforming
Uncovering
Verifying
Vetting

Showed how

Who/what?   *Skill description*   *To achieve what?*

Advising
Coaching
Conducting
Demonstrating

16

Directing
Guiding
Illustrating
Instructing
Leading
Managing
Organizing
Performing
Presenting
Teaching
Training

Set up

Who/what?	Skill description	To achieve what?
	Composing	
	Conceiving	
	Creating	
	Designing	
	Developing	
	Devising	
	Establishing	
	Founding	
	Generating	
	Implementing	
	Initiating	
	Instituting	
	Introducing	
	Inventing	
	Launching	
	Leading	
	Opening	
	Originating	
	Pioneering	
	Planning	
	Preparing	
	Producing	
	Promoting	
	Starting	

17

| | Made better | |
| Who/what? | Skill description | To achieve what? |

Broadening
Combining
Consolidating
Converting
Cutting
Decreasing
Developing
Devising
Doubling
Editing
Eliminating
Expanding
Improving
Increasing
Innovating
Minimizing
Modernizing
Recommending
Redesigning
Reducing
Refining
Reorganizing
Resolving
Restructuring
Revising
Saving
Servicing
Simplifying
Solving
Streamlining
Strengthening
Transforming
Trimming
Uncovering
Unifying
Widening

18

	Gave out	
Who/what?	Skill description	To achieve what?
	Delivering	
	Despatching	
	Distributing	
	Expanding	
	Generating	
	Launching	
	Presenting	
	Processing	
	Producing	
	Promoting	
	Providing	
	Serving	
	Transferring	

	In charge of	
Who/what?	Skill description	To achieve what?
	Administering	
	Approving	
	Conducting	
	Controlling	
	Co-ordinating	
	Directing	
	Heading	
	Leading	
	Managing	
	Representing	
	Supervising	

HOW TO USE A WINNING CV

During Application your CV is the principal weapon in your armoury. It is a *marketing tool*: what you do with it really does count and there is little point in having a winning CV but not knowing how to use it. 'The Job Market' is a well-worn term but what exactly is it and how can you identify *your* market prior to launching an all-out attack on it? Consider the following statistical breakdown of job-hunting routes:

	per cent
Advertisements	25
Agencies	20
Personal networking	30
Speculative approaches	25

This breakdown in itself means very little, but it does at least serve to show that advertised vacancies only represent a quarter of the sources of job vacancies. The rest is what we call the 'hidden job market' – those employment opportunities that do not become public knowledge through an advertisement. The above breakdown is not necessarily representitive of *your* market since other factors peculiar to you may influence the market share. Your area of specialization can be one such factor – for example, agencies traditionally take a far larger market share than 20 per cent for anyone seeking work in the hi-tech industry; probably 75 per cent of people working in this field found their job through an agency.

Age, unfortunately, has a bearing on the market. The older you are the less likely it is that your job will be found through an advertisement. Other factors may impinge but a 55-year-old job-seeker probably stands only a ten per cent chance of securing an advertised position – the market share in this case will be weighted heavily in favour of personal networking and speculative approaches (probably a combined market share of 80 per cent).

Location is another factor: the more rural a community the more insular it tends to become, and such areas cultivate vigorous 'grapevines' along which information flows. Personal networking is imperative in this environment and failure to 'plug in' to this source of inside knowledge will probably ensure an extended job search. Personal networking is not simply about approaching contacts who may be in a position to offer a job (although this can certainly be part of it). It is about making *all* your contacts aware that you are in the job market, ensuring that they are familiar with *what you are selling* (ideally by giving them a copy of your CV) and encouraging them to use *their* contacts who will in turn use *their* contacts and so on. The aim is to build up a network of people, some of whom may be well-placed to identify opportunities and feed this information back. Failure to develop your personal contacts in this way is a bit like a General omitting to tell his troops that there is a war on.

The frustration of job hunting comes from not knowing when that job offer is going to come and not knowing which sector of the market it is going to come from. Although the advertised market may only represent ten per cent of *your* market it would be short-sighted to ignore it completely. Ignoring any one of the four sectors, however unpromising it may appear, could make for an unnecessarily protracted campaign.

Beware of relying solely on agencies. This is a very common pitfall, largely because it is very reassuring to believe that some-one else is doing the work for you. You can kick up a lot of dust, and spend a lot of money, running around from one agency to another in the misguided belief that you can then sit back and await the call to an interview. The best approach is to be selective and choose those agencies which deal specifically with your specialization and salary range. Once these wheels have been set in motion, the remaining three market sectors can be concentrated on.

Concentrating on all job sources simultaneously helps to gen-erate a number of interviews *within the same time frame*. This in turn should ensure that job offers also occur over a condensed period of time, which strengthens your position, particularly when it comes to negotiating salary. This can only happen if your output of applications is itself generated within a short time frame of, say, two weeks. Attacking the whole of your market will allow you to achieve this. Adopting the passive approach of simply responding to advertisements as and when they arise will only generate one interview at a time and over an extended period of time.

A useful question to ask yourself is 'Am I spending a disproportionate amount of time on market sectors which don't justify it?' For example, if 90 per cent of your time in one week has been devoted to attacking the advertised and agency sectors (a combined 45 per cent) then this is disproportionate. Your time must be allotted to reflect the breakdown of your market as you see it.

Market sectors do, of course, overlap and the division is not always as clear as it might seem. Recruitment consultants are themselves personal contacts once you have submitted your CV and developed a relationship with them (unlike other contacts, however, they do have other clients and are not motivated by friendship). A personal contact may not be in a position to arrange a meeting/interview for you but may pass on information which leads you to make a speculative approach. An advertisement may in itself be of no use to you regarding the job advertised, but the company advertising may be of sufficient interest to prompt you to make a speculative approach.

An important rule of job hunting is that once a line of communication has been opened it should be *kept* open. Telephone personal contacts and agencies regularly to show them that you are still job hunting and are serious about it.

Action checklist

- Identify your market sectors
- Identify factors that might affect your market breakdown
- Attack 100 per cent of your market within the same time frame
- Allocate your time to reflect your market
- Be a pro-active not passive job hunter.

2 Ten hazards to overcome

Your chances of success in achieving an interview hinge on two factors:

1 How clearly the employer has defined the needs of the organization and the type of person required to fulfil those needs.

2 Your understanding of those needs and your ability to present a good case.

The more fixed the ideas an employer has on the type of person required, the more 'dangerous' your position can become. It is less dangerous for you if the needs are stated *clearly* in an advertisement: forewarned is forearmed and at least your understanding of those needs is clearer than it otherwise would be. If your application is the result of a 'speculative' approach by you then the employer's needs are less likely to be carved in tablets of stone.

When advertising a vacancy, employers are always seeking the 'ideal candidate'. They will frequently use this phrase in the advertisement itself eg, 'The ideal candidate will have . . .' In this situation it will pay you to remember that *the ideal candidate doesn't exist.* Unless the employer is extremely fortunate compromises will have to be made. How many compromises will depend upon the urgency of his or her need and the quality of the applicants. For this reason it would be inadvisable for you to dismiss out of hand any advertisement simply because you cannot satisfy *all* of the requirements. Read advertisements carefully. Take notice of the words used to describe employers' needs. Look out for words such as 'desirable' or 'preferable' which indicate that they might be willing to compromise. If you can satisfy 90 per cent of their requirements then apply for the interview.

On receipt, your CV and letter will receive no more than sixty seconds attention. In that initial sixty seconds the reader will be looking for reasons, not why they *should* see you, but why they *shouldn't* see you. This initial selection process is not one of selection at all but one of *rejection*. All applicants who *obviously* do not fit the profile will be weeded out, either rejected altogether or at the very least relegated to the 'doubtful' pile. If you have failed to emphasize your strengths and merely succeeded in highlighting your weaknesses then you have not overcome the hazards. In this section we will identify ten of the most common hazards which traditionally stop players from reaching the second stage of the game. Identification and discussion of these hazards is essential if you are to overcome them completely, or at least limit the damage they can cause.

POOR PRESENTATION

Like the way you dress for an interview, the way you present yourself on paper reflects the type of person you are. You may have all the attributes necessary to do the job but if you present them unprofessionally on paper you will not get the opportunity to sell them at an interview. It is amazing how otherwise sensible people will not think twice about spending a great deal of money on social pleasures but will be meanness personified when it comes to investing in the production of their own marketing literature. Your CV is probably the most important document you will ever have to write: it is false economy to stint on it.

In the first sixty seconds of reading your CV, a judgment will be made on you. This judgment comes before a word is read. I well remember asking an experienced personnel specialist what she looked for in a good CV. She replied that, before reading them, she would go through them much as if she were counting banknotes, and look at the *quality of the paper* used. If it was anything less than 80 gm it would immediately be consigned to the 'doubtful' pile. Now this may not sound very scientific but her rationale, based on many years of experience, has a certain logic – if applicants present themselves poorly on paper they are just as likely to present themselves poorly in person and will not be a good advertisement for the employing organization. So there it is – the first hazard encountered virtually before the game has started!

A winning CV is typed, preferably on a word processor, on good quality white A4 paper. A poorly-typed CV is little better than a hand-written one. Using a word processor has the additional benefit of allowing for changes in content should they be necessary for a 'one-off' application. Use a laser printer rather than a 'dot matrix' one – you are not printing your horoscope or biorhythm chart. Until very recently, photocopies, even on good quality paper, were not acceptable. They tended to be immediately identifiable as such and gave the recipient the impression that they were just one of many on your list. Technology has now improved to such an extent that, with a good machine, it is impossible to tell the difference between a photocopy and the original.

There is an argument, not altogether outrageous, which suggests that using paper of a different colour from white will make a CV stand out from those of the competition. Much depends on the type of job applied for – seeking a marketing or advertising position gives a little more licence to display flair or individuality, but don't overdo it.

A better way of making your application stand out from the competition is to despatch it, along with your application letter, in a stiff-backed A4 envelope. It seems a great pity to construct a winning CV only to fold it up and shove it into a losing envelope. The decision-maker may have a pile of envelopes on the desk, only one of which is A4 size. He or she is likely to open that one first if only to get it out of the way. Even if the decision-maker does not open the envelopes personally your sales literature will not be creased – all of which adds to the cumulative effect of your sales presentation.

Another way to improve your presentation and make your

CV stand out from the competition is to get rid of that ridiculously pretentious term 'Curriculum Vitae'. Losing CVs invariably have this emblazoned across the top of the page. You are not selling a Curriculum Vitae, you are selling yourself. It's much better to have your name printed in bold type and centred at the top of the document. Apart from anything else a winning CV does not really conform to the stereotyped (and now old-fashioned) style of typical Curricula Vitae. We use the term CV for convenience only and will continue to do so but you will see from the examples that winning CVs take the form of a resumé rather than a protracted historical document.

In terms of presentation your CV must be *the best example of the work you are capable of producing*. If it is anything less than that then you are not giving it enough respect, and if you don't why should others? There must be no errors of spelling or typing. If you have typed it yourself then get someone to check it for you – if you have made a mistake you will be the last person to spot it.

Pay attention to detail. For example, include your post code in your address and give your whole telephone number. Making the reader ferret about looking for your correct dialling code could be enough to put him or her off. It should go without saying that attention to detail is particularly important if the position you are seeking requires that quality. If it does the reader is bound to look for evidence of it in your application.

Above all, make sure your CV is *clear*. Winning CVs are sometimes spoiled by being too fussy. Avoid going overboard on things like underlining and superfluous use of headings such as 'name', 'address', 'status' 'nationality', 'health', 'telephone number'. They are all self-evident and your telephone number is unlikely to be mistaken for your credit card number. Apart from anything else space is at a premium because you will be aiming to get the whole of your CV on one, or at most two, sides of A4 paper – don't squander it.

Never send a photograph with your CV. A winning CV can be effectively destroyed by a losing photograph, and most photographs are just that. If the reader of your CV is desperate to get a look at you, he or she can invite you for an interview!

Presentation – hazard checklist

- Use good quality white A4 paper, minimum 100 gm
- Type, or use a word processor with a daisy wheel printer
- Put your name at centre top, not 'Curriculum Vitae'
- No spelling or typing errors
- Pay attention to detail
- Clear and concise content
- Despatch in stiff-backed A4 envelope.

TOO OLD

There is little doubt that age can be an obstacle to getting a new job. Nothing is more frustrating than knowing you have what it takes to contribute, yet being denied the opportunity because the calendar, to some, implies otherwise. The quantity and quality of talent left languishing on the employment sidelines is quite shameful. It is also perplexing, for common sense tells us that for many jobs there is little correlation between age and performance. Indeed, the older (ie more experienced) one is, the better performance is likely to be.

During Application and Interview there are certain actions you can take to limit the damage. It is really a question of saying 'Yes, age is against me but what am I going to do about it?' Firstly, it might be useful to question your own prejudices relating to age – one can be both a victim of ageism and an unknowing supporter of it. After all, the enemy is not so much age *per se* but *attitudes* towards it. These attitudes can be reflected throughout the job search. Applicants' negative attitudes about their own age are frequently detectable in their written applications. Typically, an application letter will read: 'Although I am over the age limit for this position . . .'. Such a statement can clearly indicate to the reader that the writer sees age as a problem, in which case it will be just that.

Losing CVs tend to give undue emphasis to age, marital status, number of children, nationality etc – all of which, for most jobs, should have no bearing at all on your suitability. But because they are highlighted right at the beginning the reader is almost forced to give them undue attention and is *influenced* before having had an opportunity to read the more pertinent information.

Put all personal details other than name, address and telephone number at the end of your CV unless placing them first will, for some obscure reason, increase your chances of getting an interview. Always give your date of birth rather than stating your actual age: 'Age 57' sticks out rather starkly. If age is important to the employer let him or her work it out from your date of birth.

There are more subtle ways in which age can be presented on the CV which can work against you. For example, if you make a statement to the effect that you have 'thirty years experience of production engineering' you are (quite understandably) trying to highlight your experience, but to the reader you are highlighting the fact that you are probably over fifty years of age. Trying to sell experience in terms of time is normally a big mistake: it doesn't tell the reader *how good* you are at the job, only how long you have been at it. You can also be a victim of your own pride. You may be very proud of the fact that you have 'spent a lifetime' in the shipping industry but a statement to that effect will give the reader an impression that you have already made your funeral arrangements.

Age itself isn't the problem. The problem arises from our own *prejudices* and *perceptions* about age. We tend to view anyone over a certain age as being in their *declining* years, their dotage, as being worn out with nothing to give and no enthusiasm for anything. This is clearly ludicrous, particularly as many 20-year-olds could fit that description. Your task is to avoid *reinforcing* the existing prejudices. This is done by refusing to conform to the stereotype. What you are is reflected by how you look, how you behave and by what you say. If it looks like a duck, walks like a duck and makes a noise like a duck – it is a duck.

Too old – hazard checklist

- Never apologize for your age
- Never refer to your age in an application letter
- Put all personal details at the end of the CV
- State 'Date of birth' not 'Age'
- Never sell your experience through *time*
- Project a youthful self-image.

SALARY TOO HIGH/LOW

The whole area of salary is fraught with problems and pitfalls for the unwary. In the private sector *always assume that salaries are negotiable*. A salary is either negotiable or it is not and the only way to find out is to start negotiating – but not yet. 'Don't cross your bridges before you come to them,' could well be the battle cry for all job-seekers. Putting your salary on your CV has the following risks:

1 Employers will see that your present/most recent salary is more than they are willing to pay. Although you might be willing to drop your salary (but see below) you may not get an interview to discuss the point. Employers are, not unnaturally, often reluctant to take on people at a lower salary than they were earning before. They might feel that you are using them as a 'stop gap' and will soon become disenchanted with the job, or may feel that they would be wasting your time by offering you an interview.

2 Employers will see that your present/most recent salary is a good deal less than they are willing to pay. In this case you may get through to interview but seriously weaken your bargaining position: if the salary is negotiable they are likely to use your present salary as their starting point.

3 You could be giving very misleading information. Your present salary is not in itself an accurate indication of *what the job is worth to you*. You may have perks such as a company

29

car, mortgage subsidy, free/subsidized lunches, medical insurance, non-contributory pension etc – all of which go to make up your Total Remuneration Package (TRP). Your present *salary* may be higher than the new employers can go, but their TRP may be greater than your present one. Alternatively, your present salary may be a good deal lower than the one they are offering but your TRP may be greater, particularly if there are no 'add ons' to their salary. When advertising, employers have an irritating habit of not declaring their TRP but asking you to declare yours. The financial arrangement you have negotiated with your present employer is a personal matter between you and them – strictly speaking it is no one else's business.

If you really *must* declare your salary during Application then do so on the application letter itself and not on the CV.

Dropping your salary can be a dangerous road to take. If you are changing career direction and moving from higher paid employment to what is traditionally lower paid employment eg, high technology to social work, then of course the choice is yours and if such a move satisfies your career ambitions all well and good. If, however, you are staying in the same career and you accept a substantial drop in salary this could cause problems for you in the future. What if, through no fault of your own, you find yourself back in the job market shortly afterwards? You will be job hunting again but from a weaker financial position. Your next employer will only be interested in what you are *currently* earning. As far as most employers are concerned you are only as good as your current salary/job.

Salary hazard checklist

- Always assume that salary is negotiable
- Never put your salary on your CV
- Think in terms of TRP
- Avoid taking a drop in salary.

FAILURE

Given that employers employ people to get results it naturally follows that CV evidence indicating *failure* to get results will seriously work aganst you. Nearly everyone who has had the courage to attempt something can remember at least one occasion when it hasn't worked. Failure, then, is not something to get paranoid about: it is really a question of balance and degree. Failing an examination, for example, is not the end of the world. Indeed, if you tried again, and passed, then you can get a great deal of mileage out of it – it shows that you are determined and not put off by set-backs. But the CV is the wrong place to get such selling points across – the interview is the place to do it.

Just as one swallow doesn't make a summer one failure on its own doesn't mean that *you* are a failure. A failed objective is no more than that. What is interesting is how the reader of your CV can quite easily get an impression that you are a failure by reading what are, to you, quite innocent statements. Let us look at a few:

'Marital Status: Divorced'

It is surprising how often people put this on their CV, and of course compound the error by giving it pride of place at the top! Most people regard divorce as a statement of *failure* which can instantly give you the mark of Cain. Unfair though it might seem, people have prejudices, and if the initial reader of your CV (not necessarily the interviewer) happens to have very strong feelings on the subject of divorce then *his or her* prejudice can harm your case. If you are still married then say so; if you are divorced you are 'single'; if you are separated you are married.

Misleading job titles can be harmful and may indicate failure even if you were a resounding success. Consider the following 'career pattern':

3rd job	'Assistant Supervisor'
2nd job	'Supervisor'
1st job	'Assistant Supervisor'

Now there can be a number of perfectly good reasons why you moved from 'Supervisor' *back* (?) to 'Assistant Supervisor'. Trying to give a lengthy explanation on a CV will probably do you more harm than good, but if you leave it as it is who could blame the reader for thinking 'He/she was promoted but obviously couldn't take the pace'? A job title in one company can mean something quite different in another, so have no hesitation in *changing* past job titles if you feel they might give your potential employer a totally misleading impression of you, what you did, or the circumstances surrounding your job changes. If necessary, you can explain further at the interview – if you adhere blindly to previous job titles you may not be at interviews to discuss them.

Stating that you have a 'clean driving licence' could indicate to some that at one stage it was *not* clean. 'Full driving licence' is the appropriate term (but then only necessary if it is a requirement for the job).

Think carefully before indicating that you have started something but not finished it: no one likes a 'quitter'. At the interview (should you be successful) little respect will be given to the fact that you had the initiative, enthusiasm and self-motivation to start, for example, a further education course: what *will* be questioned is the fact that you didn't finish it. As far as the CV is concerned it is worse to have started something and given up than not to have started at all.

Unfortunately, a period of self-employment can go against you. For this reason anyone thinking of starting their own business must give some thought to the potential dangers if the business should *fail*. Although it takes nerve, drive, commitment and enthusiasm to go self-employed (all qualities of interest to employers) it also takes other skills eg, planning, vision, organization, perseverance etc to make it work and get results. If your business has failed the potential employer may have reason to question those skills. In addition, he or she will be interested in your *motives* for moving from employment to self-employment and back again. The CV is not the place to raise any of this. If you are job hunting from a position of self-employment then your CV will have to make this clear, but

32

steer away from directing the reader towards *negative* factors. At the interview give your *reasons* not *excuses*.

Failure – hazard checklist

- Never put 'Divorced'
- Don't stick blindly to previous job titles
- Don't give the impression of being a 'quitter'
- Don't apologise for any period of 'failed' self-employment.

PREJUDICE

Admit it or not, we all have prejudices. We make judgments on people based upon their age, sex, appearance etc. Prejudice comes into play most strongly at an interview, but there is a particular part of the CV which can have a much stronger influence on employers than applicants think. This is the section you might call 'hobbies' or (preferably) 'interests'.

It is up to you to decide on the importance of such a section, but if you decide to include it take care, because we also judge people on their social habits and 'outside interests'. As they say in Wales 'If you play rugby or sing in a choir doors will open for you – if you do both you are destined for the top'. Many employers are interested in your activities outside the working arena because it gives them a clearer idea of the 'whole person'. Unfortunately, it can also provide the fuel to fire their prejudices. I have heard more than one employer remark that he would not choose to interview anyone who put 'golf' or 'sailing' on their CV. The rationale for this seems to be that they are both time-consuming interests and as such are incompatible with the full-time commitment expected from employees. Some prejudices arise from experience and if an employer has had a bad experience with an employee disappearing early to get to the coast then this would, not unnaturally, colour his or her feelings on this point.

A list of someone's interests can also be very boring. Many applicants put down an interest not because it is one but because they can't think of anything else to put. This is clearly ludicrous – any good interviewer would probe this at a interview and discover it to be a facade. 'Reading' is a very typical example. Unless you are seeking a job as an editor, book reviewer or proof-reader, this indicates nothing at all to your potential employer. Countless job applicants have lost their credibility at an interview through their inability to support their CV 'interests'. If you put down, say, 'reading', be prepared for the question 'Who is your favourite author?' or 'What are you reading at the moment?' If this part of your CV comes across as 'hype' an employer may well deduce that the rest of it is too.

The overall effect of your *combination* of interests can also influence the reader (for better or worse). Consider the following combinatons:

'Reading. Philately. Listening to music.'

Nothing necessarily wrong with any one of these, but should the employer be seeking someone who is a good team player then such a combination of interests might indicate otherwise. They are all *solitary* pursuits – is the applicant a loner? In addition, they could be described as somewhat *passive* which, if a certain degree of 'dynamism' is called for, might not help the applicant.

'Netball. Hockey. Swimming.'

Again, nothing particularly wrong with any of these. This person is probably a good team player and probably fairly fit but the lack of cultural pursuits might mark them down as a philistine, the importance of which would depend upon the prejudices of the reader and the type of position applied for.

'Reading. DIY. Listening to music.'

If there were a Richter Scale for measuring pure *tedium* this combination would register nine. There is nothing here which separates this person from 'Mr Average' – the complete opposite of what a winning CV should present.

'Rock climbing. Hang gliding. Free fall parachuting.'

Should this person achieve an interview one of the first questions will be 'Have you had many days off through sickness?' Remember that the customer is considering *investing* good money and no one likes to see their investment literally plummet. If the character needed to indulge in such pastimes is relevant to the job, eg, one in the SAS or as a film stunt man, then certainly include it. If, however, you are seeking something less arduous, such as area manager/salesperson, keep such pursuits to yourself – at least until you get the job.

As with any other part of the CV, the emphasis must be on *success, achievement, skills, transferable skills* or anything *relevant* which demonstrates your *uniqueness*. Consider this combination:

'School Governor. Social Club Treasurer. Successfully established Sunday league soccer team.'

This gives a revealing picture of the 'whole person' and *implies* the existence of a range of useful qualities, such as being community minded, a good 'mixer', a 'self starter', a good leader and team player, an achiever and a pro-active rather than reactive or passive person. Even if the reader does not form such a conclusion (perhaps through lack of perception or time) these are all skills/qualities which can be sold at the interview. They also provide the *evidence* which can either *support* other skills and experiences on the CV or *compensate* for the lack of them.

The basic question to ask yourself is: 'Are my activities sufficiently interesting to increase my chances of achieving an interview, or could they actually *prevent* me from doing so?' If they are unlikely to do a selling job for you, leave them out.

Prejudice – hazard checklist

- Only include interests if they will 'sell the product'
- Be aware of the 'image' your interests can project to others
- How relevant are your interests to the types of jobs for which you will be applying?
- Do your interests suggest *transferable* skills?

TOO GOOD FOR THE JOB

Being *perceived* by employers as being too 'heavyweight' for a job is arguably more frustrating than not being good enough, because of the lack of necessary feedback. Should you not be qualified/experienced enough you would normally receive a rejection letter saying so, but you will rarely get an explanation if you are *too* good. If they have declined to offer you an interview and you feel that 'being too good' is the reason then ask yourself two questions:

1 'Are they right, *am I* too good for the job?'

2 'Are they wrong but am I over selling?'

If the answer to the first question is 'yes' then the employer has probably done you a favour. You are clearly lowering your sights and in danger of taking the wrong job. What is the wrong job? It depends. You may have sound reasons for wanting to move down a few gears, but it can be quite difficult to convince employers that you really would be content to shed status and responsibility. Firstly, they might feel that after a few months you would become restless and start seeking better jobs elsewhere. Secondly, they may feel that your continued presence may become uncomfortable or even threatening – doctors don't like their nurses to be *too* intelligent.

You may, of course, not *want* to go backwards but perhaps feel you have no choice – not knowing where the next mortgage repayment is coming from can reduce your options. Looking

at it purely in terms of career progression, however, 'the wrong job' is one which gives you:
a A lower salary, and/or
b no opportunity to broaden your career.

If you take a job with either or both of the above you could be creating future problems for yourself.

If you are certain that you are *not* too 'heavyweight' for the job and that you *are* aiming at the right market then look again at your CV. 'Over selling' yourself is just as dangerous as 'under selling' but more difficult to identify. Obvious points to look out for are salary (see page 29) and job titles (page 31). Be prepared to alter job titles in a 'downwards' as well as an 'upwards' direction if you believe they might be misleading. Over the past ten years or so certain titles have become notoriously abused and devalued, eg, 'consultant', 'executive', 'director'. Your present job title may be 'Operations Director' but this could frighten off many an employer seeking an 'Operations Manager' – even though the level of responsibility could well be the same. Increasingly, employers are giving their employees fancy job titles to make them feel good, which in essence are no more than euphemisms. A 'senior sales executive' may be no more than an old salesman.

Although you must stress good selling points, be careful not to overdo it or you could easily come across as being boastful and conceited: the dividing line between confidence and 'cockiness' is very thin. Employers may interpret the words and phrases you use in an entirely unexpected way. 'Trouble shooter', for instance, is creeping into CVs quite a lot these days, but to some it is too close to 'trouble maker' for comfort.

Having too many qualifications can be just as much a hazard as having too few. This is a sound justification for putting your qualifications at the end of the CV rather than the beginning, unless, for instance, you are seeking a position in academia and are well qualified for it. Should you be the proud possessor of a PhD then for some jobs you may need to play this down rather than sell it strongly. Placing the title 'Dr' next to your name at the top can frighten as well as impress. This also applies to officers in the services seeking civilian employment. 'Major

John Brown' may be a form of address less than endearing to some civilian employers.

Applicants seeking scientific/technical/academic positions are particularly prone to being perceived as 'too heavyweight' by employers. This perception is often unwittingly encouraged by such applicants through their insistence upon detailing every item of equipment used and every published paper. These are, of course, important details, so important in some cases that the offer of an interview may hinge on their inclusion, but keep such information *separate*. Do not allow it to invade the CV itself.

Training courses can also hinder rather than help an application. It is not unusual for applicants to include on their CV a list of training courses they have attended when working for previous employers. This in itself is not necessarily a hazard since many courses are very useful and extremely expensive. Potential employers may, then, be very relieved to escape the expense of sending an applicant on a particular course. But this can be a double-edged sword. The list of courses attended by some applicants is often so extensive that the employer cannot but wonder how little time the applicant actually spent at work. 'Professional course attenders' are a well recognized breed of job applicant. If you are tempted to include such information then question the importance/relevance of each course and be selective.

Too good for the job – hazard checklist

- Question whether you are lowering your sights
- Don't mention salary
- Beware of pretentious job titles and phrases
- Consider 'playing down' professional titles
- Omit peripheral activities.

LACK OF EXPERIENCE

Indicating that you do not have the necessary experience for the job is frequently no more than the result of selling the wrong things on your CV. The reader is, more precisely, looking for *relevant* experience, ie particular aspects of your past/present experience which are likely to be useful in *fulfilling his or her needs*. Losing CVs have an alarming tendency to confuse the reader by drawing attention to *irrelevancies*. These irrelevancies act as a smoke screen which, particularly in long-winded CVs, hides the fact that you do indeed have relevant experience.

For example, many applicants unwittingly make the mistake of selling their *previous employers* rather than themselves. Much valuable space is devoted to giving a blow by blow account of a previous employer's strategy, restructuring/reorganizing, acquisitions and policy, all of which might be interesting should the reader have the time and inclination to read it, but bears no direct relevance at all to the applicant's suitability for the job. In addition, inadvertently giving away privileged information about previous employers is unlikely to endear you to potential employers – they may offer you an interview to find out even more about their competitors but you will pay the price for your indiscretion.

Irrelevancies can also creep in if you are moving from one 'industry' to another quite different one. If, for example, your most recent experience has entailed the selling of kitchen furniture and you are seeking a position selling televisions, radios etc, then peppering your CV with references to refrigerators, freezers and washing machines is unlikely to enhance your case. That you have experience of selling one type of goods is not *immediately* and *directly* relevant to where *you want to be*, ie selling televisions and radios. The relevant and common factor is that you have successfully sold consumer products – so it is the words 'consumer products' which should appear on the CV and not references to the products themselves. Steer away from any references which may encourage the reader to say 'We are not in that line of business, therefore this is all irrelevant experience'.

Getting the fact that you have relevant experience across

requires you to be *clear* and *concise*. Refuse to hide behind 'woolly' words and phrases which continually seem to crop up on CVs but which mean very little to the reader – words like 'Wide', 'Broad', 'Involved', 'Dealing with . . .' How wide? How broad? How were you involved? How did you 'deal with' customer problems? Did you resolve them? What skills did you use in resolving them?

If the right job is one which allows you to broaden your career then by definition it must give you something *new*. This means that it must allow you to undertake new responsibilities which give you *new* experiences which in turn give you *new* skill(s) and the opportunity to *achieve* new things. It naturally follows that you should be seeking a job *for which you do not possess all of the experience* (although, as we have said, you may already possess the *skill* to do it). Looking at it another way, if you are applying for a position for which you have *all* of the required experience, then you are probably going for the *wrong* job. For this reason, you should not be unduly concerned by the experience you *lack* as long as you can sell the experience you *have*. When you get to the interview you can really make 'lack of experience' work for you. For example:

Q. 'We were really looking for someone with experience of dealing with the public – you don't have this do you?'
A. 'No, I'm afraid I don't.'

This clearly won't do – you are simply confirming their worst fears. What you could say is:

A. 'Well, in a way that is the reason I am here today. Although
   I can satisfy most of the things you are looking for I am very
   keen to take on this responsibility. I am confident that I have
   the necessary ability and personal qualities to do that part of
   the job extremely well.'

Here, you are *reassuring* the interviewer that, despite your lack of direct experience, you have the confidence, enthusiasm, ability and desire to do the job. You are clearly unafraid by the prospect.

Highlighting irrelevancies on the CV will also happen if you give too much importance to your earliest jobs. Employers are only likely to be interested in what you have been doing during the past few years: the further back you go the less relevant your experience is likely to be. It is only necessary to give the name of your employer and a job title for earlier jobs.

Because your most recent work is likely to be the most relevant you must give it priority. This means that (unless you have a valid reason for doing otherwise) your career progression must be outlined in *reverse* chronological order, ie your most recent job *first* and working backwards through to your earliest job. Making the reader wade through twenty years of irrelevancies can seriously diminish the appetite for reading any further.

There is no doubt then that lack of relevant experience can impair your chances of getting an interview, and often rightly so – either you have enough of the right experience or you don't. But candidates often fail at this hurdle, not because they don't have the requisite amount of relevant experience but through their failure to sell it in the right way. Who can blame a busy employer for failing to reach the right conclusion in sixty seconds?

Lack of experience – hazard checklist

- Don't sell irrelevant experience
- Don't sell your employers
- Be specific. Don't use vague descriptions
- Sell the experience you *have* – not the experience you lack
- Describe jobs in reverse chronological order.

JOB HOPPER

Changing employers every three to five years or so does not necessarily impair your future prospects. Personal career management is all about making the right moves at the right time and for the right reasons. If you are fortunate enough to stay with the same employer *and* broaden your experience, learn new skills and achieve new objectives then that is ideal. Unfortunately this is not always possible. If your career is not developing quickly enough with your present employer, you must *take control* of it and be determined enough to achieve your objectives elsewhere.

Remaining in the same job for more than five years can cause problems for you in the future, particularly if you are unceremoniously thrown into the job market through redundancy. Prospective employers are likely to deduce from your CV that your career ceased developing some time ago and that you are probably suffering from 'career inertia' – the direct opposite of personal career management.

Although you may have changed employers quite regularly the 'job hopping' criticism will be levelled at you only if it is clear that there is *no logical pattern* to your moves. In these circumstances employers may conclude that you are shiftless, indecisive, lacking in direction and a square peg who always seems to squeeze into a round hole. Such criticism can, of course, be very unfair. Fate does sometimes deal a poor hand and such things as changing family circumstances can override and damage career objectives. Most sensible employers would not worry unduly about one period of employment outside your chosen career path. Few people are fortunate enough to select the right career from leaving school; others go through what might be called 'the career menopause' when the desire to briefly break free from the constricting chains of a chosen career proves irresistible.

Job hopping is about *consistent* career abuse, ie when consecutive job changes bear no identifiable relation to each other. If you *are* a job hopper the good news is that it isn't a terminal disease. You simply haven't found the right vehicle through which your latent abilities and potential can be tapped. But from a practical point of view there is little you can do to indicate this on your CV – in one way or another you must tell employers where you have worked, what you did and when.

The more job changes you have had (whether logical or

otherwise) the more 'messy' your CV is likely to look. This danger can be offset by giving less priority to dates of employment. Traditionally, CVs have tended to place undue emphasis on this by putting dates of employment down the left hand side of the page. Because we read from left to right it is the dates we see first. This can lead to instant confusion and detract from the more pertinent information. A winning CV is one which has the dates on the right hand side of the page. After all, *what* you have done is more relevant than when you did it.

Your desire not to be seen as a job hopper may tempt you to state your 'reasons for leaving' previous jobs, but why you left one employer and joined another is a bridge to be crossed at the interview: it is easier to explain your motives at a face to face meeting. If you *must* give such reasons during Application make sure they don't damage your case. If you left because of a personality clash or for anything other than positive reasons, then a statement to that effect can reflect badly upon you, albeit unfairly.

Be cautious about including 'objectives' or 'position sought' on the CV. There is nothing essentially wrong in doing this for 'one-off' CVs aimed at a particular job as you can tailor your objective to it. For a general purpose CV, however, it is infuriating to see an 'objective' which does not really fit the bill at any given time. If you do have an objective which can fit every situation it is likely to be so vague as to be useless.

However, because job hopping is a sign that one has perhaps in the past had no clear objective, it can be a good idea to compensate for this by stating clearly and confidently what your objective is *now*. This encourages the reader to say: 'He now seems to know what he wants even though he hasn't achieved it in the past.'

One useful way of minimizing the risk of being seen as a 'job hopper' is to use the 'Functional' style of CV (see Part 4). This hits prospective employers with your skills etc before they are aware that you have been around a bit. If necessary the names and relevant dates of employers/employment can be given on a completely separate sheet.

Job hopper – hazard checklist

- Put all dates on the right hand side
- Do not explain your 'reasons for leaving'
- Consider stating your objective
- Consider using the functional style of CV.

TOO YOUNG

Being considered 'too young' for a job is just as much of an anachronism as being considered too old. It is meaningless in the context of employment: either one is *competent* enough to do the job or one is not. Lack of skill or ability can render 'young' and 'old' applicants incompetent but age itself does not. Some jobs, for instance, require a level of maturity not often found in someone below a certain age. A problem arises because some employers, through their own prejudices and preconceptions, believe that maturity/ability can *never* be found in someone below a certain age. During an interview a 'young' applicant can challenge those prejudices and change the perceptions – unfortunately, the interview may not be forthcoming *because* of that prejudice.

Once you are inside an organization and seeking promotion it is easier to change the perceptions of others – getting results is one of the strongest arguments against entrenched attitudes. If you *do* lack the maturity/ability/skill required by the employer, this will inevitably show up in your application letter and CV. If you don't lack maturity/ability/skill then you should be able to produce the quality of written work to suggest as much. This is done not by referring in any way to your age (that would be just highlighting a 'weakness') but by displaying *belief* and projecting a confident self-image. As with the 'too old' hazard it is a matter of refusing to conform to the stereotype. In this case the stereotyped application would be one which is servile and lacking in conviction.

44

THE 'EMPTY TAXI'

'An empty taxi pulled up and the applicant got out.'

Perhaps the biggest hazard of all is the 'empty taxi' CV. This is a CV which conveys nothing to the reader – at least, nothing which will encourage them to recommend an interview. In a sense it is a combination of some or all of the other hazards. A winning CV should convey the message: 'Look at me, I am worth seeing.'

The 'empty taxi' conveys a quite different message: 'I'm only applying on the off-chance that you might see me – then I will *really* be able to tell you how bad I am.'

The 'empty taxi' applicant lacks assurance and fails to reassure the reader. Before Application gets under way you should devote some time to self-analysis. This will help you to understand *who* you are and what your needs are in terms of a job. After all, job hunting is an opportunity to fulfil personal needs. Once this is achieved, the emphasis *during* Application must shift towards showing a greater understanding and awareness of *the needs of the employer*. For many applicants such a shift fails to take place: the job search during both Application and Interview remains self-centred and this is reflected in CVs and application letters. An unacceptable number of letters, for example, contain the 'I want' and 'I am looking for' phrases which are anathema to anyone involved in recruitment.

A good employer will, of course, be interested in your needs in terms of career objectives and salary. But these matters will only be addressed once he or she has received clear signals from you that you have *something to offer*. Empty taxis fail to convey these signals.

To understand the importance of this is to realize the one fundamental need possessed by all recruiters, ie the need to keep *their* job. Those charged with the onerous responsibility of selecting the right person are required to tread a thin and sometimes precarious line. Not all are trained in those techniques designed to increase the probability of selecting round pegs for round holes. Getting it right is their primary objective, largely

45

because the cost of getting it wrong is loss of credibility from peers and senior staff and, if it happens too often, loss of a job. This applies just as much to recruitment agencies. They are paid by employers to select and recommend suitable applicants; they need to get it right because they want those employers to continue providing them with business.

The customer, whether employer or agency, therefore needs *reassurance* from you, *in writing*, that you have what it takes to fulfil his or her needs. Early on in the selection process, the customer (who may be represented by someone quite junior in the organization) rejects all those applications which fail the reassurance test. It is at this stage that all the empty taxis are sidelined.

Clearly then, it is not good enough for you to write a 'pleasant' letter of application – this in itself is no justification for the interview. The reader needs hard facts to present to superiors, and must be able to say 'I think we should interview this person *because. . . .*'

3 Putting it all together

PRESENTING THE FACTS

Constructing a winning CV requires you to achieve two objectives:

1 Putting the factual information together in a presentable and readable form.
2 Ensuring that this factual information illustrates the good things about you and eliminates anything which might restrict your chances of getting through to the interview.

The factual information represents the 'skeleton' of the CV eg, dates, places and names. It is the essence of 'what you have done'. This is unlikely to present you with any real problems and is more of a chore than anything else. But once completed it is the frame upon which you hang the second objective, which 'puts flesh on the bare bones'.

The following 'Worksheets', for you to complete, should enable you to achieve the first objective as painlessly as possible. To achieve the second objective refer back to the Skills analysis exercise on pages 12–19.

Worksheet 1 – Education history

School	Qualification	From	To

College	Qualification	From	To

University/Polytechnic	Qualification	From	To

Evening classes:			
Adult education centre/ College of further ed.	Subject/qual	From	To
Training:			
Place of training	Course Title	From	To

Worksheet 2 – Employment history

(Most recent job first)

Employer		From To
Location		Job title
Functions/what did I do?		
1.		
2.		
3.		
4.		
5.		
6.		
7.		
8.		
9.		
10.		

Employer		From	To
Location		Job title	

Functions/what did I do?

1.

2.

3.

4.

5.

6.

7.

8.

9.

10.

Employer		From	To
Location	·	Job title	

Functions/what did I do?

1.

2.

3.

4.

5.

6.

7.

8.

9.

10.

Employer			From	To
Location			Job title	

Functions/what did I do?

1.

2.

3.

4.

5.

6.

7.

8.

9.

10.

Employer		From	To
Location		Job title	

Functions/what did I do?

1.

2.

3.

4.

Employer		From	To
Location		Job title	

Functions/what did I do?

1.

2.

3.

4.

Worksheet 3 – CV layout

```
┌─────────────────────────────────────────┐
│ 1. Name                                  │
└─────────────────────────────────────────┘

┌──────────────────┐   ┌──────────────────────────┐
│ 2. Address       │   │ 3. Telephone             │
│                  │   └──────────────────────────┘
│                  │
└──────────────────┘

   ┌───────────────────────────────────────┐
   │ 4. Profile                            │
   └───────────────────────────────────────┘

   ┌──────────────────────────────┐
   │ 5. Key skills                │
   └──────────────────────────────┘

┌──────────────────────────────────┐  ┌─────────────┐
│ 6. Career                        │  │ 7. Dates    │
│                                  │  │             │
│                                  │  │             │
│                                  │  │             │
│                                  │  │             │
│                                  │  │             │
│                                  │  │             │
└──────────────────────────────────┘  └─────────────┘

┌───────────────────────────────────────────┐
│ 8. Education                              │
└───────────────────────────────────────────┘

┌──────────────────────────────────┐
│ 9. Personal                      │
└──────────────────────────────────┘

┌──────────────────────────────────┐
│ 10. Interests                    │
└──────────────────────────────────┘
```

THE TEN ELEMENTS AND ACTION CHECKLIST

	Action
1 Name	• Print your name in *bold type* at centre top of CV.
	• No need to use your full or legal Christian name. Use the name you wish to be addressed by at the interview.
2 Address	• Top left of CV or directly beneath your name at centre.
	• Pay attention to detail – include your post code.
3 Telephone/Fax /e mail	• Top right of CV
	• Give the full dialling code number.
	• Give your work and home numbers if you can.
4 Profile	• Make it brief – no more than two sentences.
	• Does it describe you accurately – a good pen picture?
	• Does it give the reader an indication of where you want to be in terms of a job?
5 Key skills	• Be selective – no more than six key skills.
	• Give the priority to more important/ relevant skills.
	• Use the right 'action words' to describe the skills.
	• Do not include dates.
	• Remember the importance of *transferable* skills.
6 Career	• Start with your present/most recent job and work backwards.

- Use 'telex-style' sentences – cut the 'waffle'.
- Quantify when appropriate.
- Arouse curiosity.
- Do not use misleading job titles.
- Cut out 'jargon' or 'buzz words'.
- Use positive words eg, 'success' 'achievement'.
- Give less space to irrelevant early jobs.

7 Dates
- Put all dates on the right hand side.
- Only put the years eg, '1978–82' – exact dates are irrelevant and untidy.
- Do not leave years unaccounted for.

8 Education
- Omit examination failures.
- Give priority to the most relevant qualifications eg, if you have a degree there is no need to spell out each 'O' level qualification.
- Be selective about training courses attended.

9 Personal
- Marital status 'married' or 'single' – not 'divorced'.
- Put 'date of birth' not 'age'.

10 Interests (optional)
- Only include interests which are *different, intriguing*, or which indicate transferable skills, achievements or responsibilities.
- Assess the overall effect of your interests (see pages 33–36).

STEP-BY-STEP CONSTRUCTION OF A WINNING CV

The objective is to get your CV on one or two sheets of A4 paper, but don't worry about this at first – your first rough draft can be as long as you like, the editing will come later. Begin with your 'career' (element number six) and the appropriate dates (element number seven). Start with your present/most recent job and work backwards. At this stage give free rein to your thoughts and even include what you think *might* be irrelevant – at this early stage it is better to include everything rather than be too selective too soon and risk throwing the baby out with the bath water.

Analyse and dissect your jobs carefully. Break your job functions down to their smallest components. As your most recent jobs are likely to be more relevant you should have more to say about them.

Once you have completed your draft, begin *editing*. Take out anything which is clearly irrelevant, ie anything which *will not help you get to where you want to be*. Avoid repetition: you only need to mention a particular skill once.

Get rid of any superfluous words. Avoid the continuous narrative form of writing. The body of the CV should consist of short, sharp sentences or statements. Keep use of the first person singular (ie '*I* did this and then *I* did that') to a minimum. Overuse is boring, a waste of space and unnecessary. After all, it is obvious that the CV is about you so there's no point in repeating it. It should be almost as if you are writing about someone else. Never write in the past tense, even when describing previous employment, ie 'produced reports for senior management'. The 'ing' action words (see pages 13–19) can give an old job much more immediacy and relevance, ie 'producing reports for senior management'. Remember to include successes and achievements, and to quantify where appropriate.

What you leave out is in many ways just as important as what you choose to include. You are fishing for an interview and the CV is your bait. Do not overload the hook. You want the reader to say 'I must see this person to find out *more*,' so

58

don't tell the whole story. Try to introduce an element of intrigue to arouse curiosity. For example:

'Devising unique system of stock control now used by all UK outlets – making savings of £50,000 per annum.'

Think carefully about whether you have made changes or suggestions which have increased efficiency and effectiveness and saved your employer *money*. If you have then say so, but don't give a blow by blow account: this leaves an employer with no reason to see you.

Having analysed and edited your past jobs you will now be in a stronger position to tackle element five, which should list no more than half a dozen *key skills*. Do not confuse skills with responsibilities, experience or achievements. (If in doubt refer back to 'What Are You Selling?' pages 4–12) The great advantage in having this element is that dates are not included. If appropriate a key skill can come from your earliest job or an outside interest. If you *are* short on specific skills, as a school-leaver might be, then certainly use this element to describe other attributes or personal qualities.

Using the Action Checklist on pages 56–57, you can now complete elements 1, 2, 3, 7, 8, 9, 10 of your CV.

Element four, the 'Profile', is arguably the most important element, if for no other reason than that it will be *studied* first. The completion of this is best left until last. It should give the reader a 'thumb nail' sketch of you as a 'whole person'. It must be a statement which includes what you consider are the *most important* facts about yourself. For this reason there are no limits in terms of *what* you choose to include. You may include skills, experience, achievements, responsibility, job title (but not necessarily one given to you by a previous employer) or personal qualities. In effect it is a summary of all the other elements. The following are examples of profiles:

'Experienced and versatile Warehouseman and skilled fork lift driver.'

'Stockbroker/Solicitor with international, financial, contractual and legal experience.'

'Experienced and flexible Secretary with word processing, short-hand and language skills.'

'A conscientious, enthusiastic and well-presented Personal Secretary with experience at a senior level within the financial sector.'

'Seven years experience in different office environments. Sound keyboard skills. Ability and interest to learn new computer system.'

Note that it is not necessary to pin a label on yourself – there's no point in describing yourself as a secretary if that is not where you want to be. It is also pointless to emphasize that you have 'experience in the financial sector' if you want to move away from that sector.

Having completed all the elements, get the CV typed. Have someone check it for you to identify spelling/typing errors. Can you get it all on one side of A4? Don't try to squeeze it all in if it won't go. As a rough guide there should be more 'white' on the page than 'black'. If you must go on to a second sheet then spread the elements out so that you *use* two whole sheets: one and a half sides looks unbalanced.

Check your CV for *hazards* (Refer back to Part 2). Eliminate anything which is likely to stop you from getting an interview.

Finally, use the 'Cringe Factor'. Does your CV make you cringe just a little with embarrassment? If so you probably have a winning CV.

4 The good, the bad and the indifferent

INTRODUCTION

There are widely differing views on what constitutes a winning CV. The fact that even 'experts' can disagree about how a first class CV should be constructed is not surprising since there can be no set format. Why? Because no two applicants are identical and each CV should be as unique as a fingerprint. This part of the book is therefore not designed to impose a set format, and the examples of winning CVs are no more than that – although you will see, for the reasons given in the preceding chapters, that they have much in common.

It is by no means impossible for you to construct your own CV and this book is designed to help you do just that. But you will find it difficult to be objective – self-portraits are notoriously unreliable. Do show your draft CV to someone whose opinion you respect and who is likely to be able to offer an objective viewpoint. It is quite useless for someone else to do it for you. CVs by post tend to throw up a Frankenstein's Monster – more of an identikit picture than a representative portrait. The best CVs are produced as the result of a joint effort between yourself and a professional at a face-to-face meeting.

In this part we will be looking at some examples of losing CVs and winning CVs. The merits of each one are discussed in a brief critique, designed to make you consider whether the recommendations are appropriate to *your situation*. They are no more than suggested guidelines from which you may wish to work. They are not to be taken lightly but neither are they carved in tablets of stone. It is no use ending up with a CV in which you have no confidence, so be prepared to follow your own intuition.

As all the examples are taken from actual case studies, all information which might lead to identification has been changed.

CASE STUDY 1

Curriculum Vitae

Personal

Name: Roger Hall   Date of Birth: 18.9.58

Address: 17 Stone Street   Status: Divorced
        Windsor
        Bucks. WD4 7JF

Telephone no. (01552) 837452   General Health: Good

Education

1969–76   Upper Windsor Comprehensive

Qualifications:

'O' Level	Grade
English Literature	B
English Language	B
Mathematics	C
History	A
Geography	B
Physics	B
Chemistry	B

'A' Level	
English Literature	B
History	A
Geography	B

Case study 1 was only the first page of a six-page CV. Roger went on to university and achieved a 2:1 honours degree, in which case there is no point at all in spelling out each 'O' and 'A' Level, let alone the grades (good though they were). '7 O & 3 A Levels' would have been perfectly adequate and saved two thirds of a page of A4. Subsequent academic success often makes previous examination results, if not irrelevant, certainly of less importance. Because of this Roger's CV lacks *impact*.

There was also ten years of experience, achievements and skills tucked away on the remaining five pages. Roger was selling the wrong things.

Medical bulletins are unnecessary. It is normally assumed that your state of health is A1 unless you state otherwise at the interview. (Some jobs of course require you to undertake a medical examination before the job offer is confirmed.) If applicants *must* make a health statement on the CV they should put 'Health: Excellent'. Roger's health was also excellent but because he put 'Good' employers might have thought there was something wrong with him!

The 'failure' hazard (see page 31) is identifiable here. Remember, if you are divorced then you are single.

The term 'Curriculum Vitae' is now 'old hat'. Put your *name* at centre top.

CASE STUDY 2

TRACY FULLERTON

127 Garside Avenue
Whitchurch
Manchester
MC9 4EL

Home: 01372 921674

Work: 01372 546021

A CLERICAL OFFICER/VDU OPERATOR with experieence
in warehousing, finance and exporting.

Key skills/attributes:

* Typing and accurate operation of VDU terminals
* Inputting and controlling incoming and outgoing products
  (high throughput)
* Reconciling stock on a daily basis on computerised system
* Reliable, trustworthy, excellent attendance record

Budget Electronics (UK) Limited   1989–96

Typist/VDU Operator

– Responsible for telephone queries from customers/colle-
  agues on delivery and stock positions.
– Operated VDU terminals for inputting/retrieval of informa-
  tion/statistics.
– Checked and collated documents for deliveries on a daily
  basis.
– Checked and collated documents for deliveries on a daily
  basis.
– Typing and filing of general correspondence for senior
  managers.

PG Trust Group Limited   1983–89

Branch Clerk

– General office duties including typing and filing.
– Operated busy VDU terminal.
– Dealt with expenses/subsistence of representatives.

United Asia Company Limited   1981–83

Export Shipping Clerk

– Checked availability of containers and container space.
– Arranged haulage to port of embarkation.
– General office, typing and VDU duties.

EDUCATION

CSE: 7 including Mathematics, English and Typing

PERSONAL

Date of birth: 16.4.65   Status: Single

INTERESTS

Horse riding, keeping fit, charity fund raising.

Case study 2 is a very good attempt at a winning CV but lack of professionalism has quickly turned it into a losing one. Tracy sells, among her other skills and attributes, 'accurate operation of VDU terminals'. This is a proud boast but the reader can, on two occasions, see *evidence to the contrary* on the CV itself:

1. '. . . . ./VDU OPERATOR with experieence . . .'
2. 'Checked and collated documents . . .' is repeated by mistake.

Tracy has obviously not checked accurately her own marketing literature. Who then can blame an employer for deducing that she is not as accurate as she thinks she is? The result is a potentially winning CV spoiled by slipshod presentation (see pages 24–27).

A good effort has been made to use the right 'action words' but there is a lack of consistency in the tense used. Always write in the present tense ie 'operating', 'checking', even when describing past jobs.

On two occasions, a skill description is *vague*:

1 'Responsible for telephone queries . . .'
Turn again to the 'Skills analysis exercise' (pages 12–19). Under the vague description 'talked to', what Tracy was really doing was '*Advising* customers/colleagues on delivery and stock positions, and *resolving* queries'.
2 'Dealt with expenses/subsistence . . .'
In the same exercise the closest vague description to 'Dealt with' is 'Sorted out'. Look under the skill description column for the most accurate word which describes what Tracy was actually doing. She was probably 'collating', 'itemizing' or 'assessing' expenses/subsistence of representatives'. She may even have been 'approving' them which is a different and more important experience altogether: 'In charge of'.

The 'profile' Tracy has chosen is interesting because the title 'Clerical Officer' does not appear as one of her previous job titles. This is quite correct if she sees herself as more than just a typist. Her current or last job title, 'Typist/VDU Operator', appears to be more than a little misleading as there is a strong clerical bias to the responsibilities of the job.

CASE STUDY 3

BRIAN WATTS

28 Sudbury Drive
Horley Park
Teignton
Bristol BS2 6JL   01497 784361

CLASS 3 HGV DRIVER with experience of delivering durable and non-durable products throughout the UK.

EXPERIENCE

HOYLAKE ELECTRONICS Plc – Teignton   1974–96

- Delivering safely electronic products valued at up to £400,000 per load. Averaging 37,000 miles per year without accident.
- Assisting the Route Planner to advise on time/cost effective routes.
- Ensuring that complex documentation for transfer of products is completed accurately.
- Establishing excellent relationship with customers and representing the company in a professional manner.
- Carrying out daily comprehensive checks on vehicle to ensure compliance with safety legal standards and trouble free operation.

ABCO STORES LTD – Brighton   1967–74

- Driving HGV Class 1 and Class 3 vehicles delivering to shops, supermarkets and warehouses nationally.
- Gaining warehouse and fork truck experience.

RWB DAIRIES Ltd – Brighton   1961–67

- Delivering milk and dairy products. Collecting, balancing and banking cash (£575 weekly average).

PERSONAL

Date of Birth: 4.1.45   Married. 2 children

Case study 3 is a winning CV. What is encouraging about this is that Brian does not see himself as 'just a lorry driver'. He is clearly proud of his skills and has made a good attempt at selling them. As a variation on a theme, notice that Brian has chosen to write his skill statements, not under a separate heading beneath the profile but as an integral part of his career history. This is perfectly acceptable and can save a lot of unnecessary repetition.

Because his education at school was very basic he has chosen not to sell it at all – quite rightly as it is not relevant. He does make the point that he is sufficiently intelligent to cope with complex documentation – that is what matters to prospective employers.

Brian *quantifies* wherever he can, ie '£400,000 per load', '37,000 miles per year', '£575 weekly average'. Notice also how he 'plays down' the type of products he delivers. To an employer wanting him to deliver garden furniture the fact that he has delivered radio and television sets would be irrelevant. He might have improved upon this by using the term 'perishable products' instead of 'milk and dairy products' (it is self-evident anyway) but he does make the point right at the beginning that he has experience of durable and non-durable products.

CASE STUDY 4

PETER HARRISON

432 London Road
Bedford
BD5 9FD   01427 748826

Adaptable and conscientious HGV Class 1 Driver wth 29 years experience of accident-free driving.

QUALIFICATIONS:

CERTIFICATE OF PROFESSIONAL COMPETENCE
ADVANCED HEAVY GOODS VEHICLE DRIVER
CLASS 1 HEAVY GOODS VEHICLE LICENCE
HAZARDOUS CHEMICALS CERTIFICATE

EXPERIENCE

Heavy Haulage:

* Loading/driving abnormal loads
* Liaising with police traffic control to plan movement orders
* Skilled in use of low loaders, dolly and rear steering, mobile cranes

Multi-drop Deliveries:

* Maintaining good customer relations at all sites, depots and shops visited
* Collecting cash payments/completing documentation
* Planning economic routes

Bulk load trunking:

* Operating day/night to and from depots, bonded warehouses and shops
* Carrying and ensuring safety of loads valued up to £50,000
* Night trunking chemicals tankers

EMPLOYMENT RECORD

BENSONS Ltd – Bedford	1987–96
KOLDSTORE Ltd – Glasgow	1982–87
BASSETT MULTI-LINE – Glasgow	1974–82
HARRISON GROUP Ltd – Glasgow	1968–74
HYDROCHEM Ltd – Edinburgh	1964–68

MILITARY SERVICE – ROYAL SIGNALS   1958–64

PERSONAL

Date of Birth: 12.6.42   Single   Health: Excellent

Case study 4 is also a winning CV. Although Peter has chosen to sell skills, experience, achievements and attributes in a very different way, it pays off. This is a useful example to show how the format can be varied while sticking to the rules of the 'application game'. Peter sees his professional qualifications (as opposed to his educational qualifications) as a primary selling point and has accordingly elected to give these prominence.

He does leave himself open to the hazard 'too old' by selling experience through time, ie '29 years experience of accident-free driving'. The reader is immediately encouraged by this to look for the date of birth to see how old he is. However, this is probably the exception to the rule as the fact that he has such a good driving record and breadth of experience should compensate for the age factor. Perhaps in an attempt to allay any fears on this front Peter has decided to make a health statement at the end of the CV.

Cleverly, he avoids giving a blow by blow account of each job by categorizing his experience under three headings. This is an excellent way of selling *relevant* and avoiding *irrelevant* information. He makes little mention of the actual products he was involved with although they are hinted at – he can elaborate on this *as necessary* in the accompanying letter. He is truly selling his experience through skills.

Under 'EMPLOYMENT RECORD' you will see 'HARRISON GROUP Ltd' – this is *intriguing*. Perhaps this was a period of self-employment: it is undoubtedly something to be raised at the interview.

CASE STUDY 5

BILL JOHNSTONE

62 Methuen Road
Horndean
Worcester
WC4 6FS   01833 653214

CAREER

BLACKWOOD ELECTRICS Ltd – Worcester   1984–Present

Chief Security Manager responsible for total security of 9 acre high risk warehouse and distribution site employing 275 personnel with stock valued at up to £70 million.

– Supervising 6 security officers and organising shift rotas to provide 24 hour security cover.
– Organizing site fire drills. Liaising with Chief Fire Officer and carrying out joint site inspections. Maintaining fire equipment.
– Maintained First Aid and Ambulance facilities. Investigated all accidents and identified safety hazards.
– Carried out random/regular personal and vehicle searches.
– Investigated incidents liaising with police and management.

HOMELEIGH GROUP Ltd – Hereford   1981–84

Security and First Aid Officer supervising 3 security and 2 ambulance room staff.
– Working on a three shift system.
– Looking after on site car parking.

WATSON & HUGHES Ltd – Liverpool   1974–81

Demolition Supervisor

– Demolition of factories (mainly steel).
– Training 9 men in safety and hazard identification.
– Looking after burning equipment and oxy-acetaline.

73

TFF HOLDINGS LTD – Liverpool   1964–74

Caulker Burner

– Operating electronic burning machines.

NATIONAL SERVICE – Paratrooper and Medic   1961–64

SEWARD CONSTRUCTION Ltd – Glasgow   1956–61

Shipyard Worker

PERSONAL

Date of Birth: 4.8.40   **Single**   **Full driving licence**

Case study 5 is not exactly a losing CV but one which could have been improved with a little more thought.

Much will of course depend upon the type of job Bill is seeking. He might feel that his age limits his options and this might be the reason why he has chosen not to include a profile. He puts his experience in security and safety in a prominent position on his CV, so we must assume then that this is the area in which he will be concentrating his search. This being the case a profile stating that he is 'A fully experienced Security/Safety specialist with supervisory and management skills' would have told the reader where he was coming from and given a stronger indication of where he wanted to be. It would have given the CV more *conviction* and at the same time played down the fact that he is currently a Chief Security Manager (thus avoiding the 'too experienced' hazard).

Bill could have made room for the profile by eliminating the descriptions of his duties as a 'Demolition Supervisor' and 'Caulker Burner'. The job titles would have sufficed since the safety implications of those jobs should be self-evident. He is very unlikely to move back into the demolition business, so there's no point in making a meal of it.

Bill uses the right action words but (like so many others) slips back into the past tense (from 'Supervis*ing*' and 'Organiz*ing*' to 'Maintain*ed* and 'Investigat*ed*'). 'Carried out random/regular personal and vehicle searches' is left as a vague statement. What does this mean? How accurate a description is it of what Bill did? As the Chief Security Manager one would have expected his six security officers to have *carried out* the searches. As Bill was in charge of the operation look at 'In charge of' experience in the Skills analysis exercise on pages 12–19. 'Directing random/regular personal and vehicle searches' is probably a much more accurate and effective description of what he was doing. If you select the wrong word then the reader will *read* the wrong word. This in turn will leave them with an inaccurate description of what you did.

CASE STUDY 6

ELIZABETH HALL

9 Copythorn Drive
Longdon Estate
Lingfield
Kent. KT1 4PU

Work: 0171 978954

Home: 01342 364761

An innovative, accurate and versatile DESK TOP PUBLISHER seeking Supervisory position.

Key Skills Include:

* Defining/setting formats for all work prior to publication
* Liaising with management/senior staff and recommending layout
* Excellent technical and practical knowledge of Pagemaker, Word, MacWrite, MacDraw, Paint, Cricket Graph and Formation packages running on Apple Macintosh. Ventura running on IBM

CAREER

BRADWELL LAYTON Ltd – London   1991–Present

Desk Top Publishing Supervisor producing documents/reports including graphics/freehand drawings using several packages running on Apple Macintosh. Joining as DTP Operator in Word Processing Department but within 5 weeks promoted to Supervisor. Establishing separate DTP Department. Identifying, negotiating and purchasing new equipment to the value of £90k. Interviewing, selecting and training 7 additional staff.

Production Assistant to Sales Team providing Dealing Room support to 3 salesmen and 6 analysts. Controlling layout and production of UK magazine. Establishing/maintaining complex filing system and supplying back up to ensure smooth daily running of team. Researching UK companies and proof reading.

GENERAL BANK INTERNATIONAL – London 1988–91

Shorthand Secretary to team of 7 Computer Audit Managers. Producing reports and spreadsheets. Advising/assisting and resolving word processing/printing problems of 5 other secretaries.

BT INTERNATIONAL – London   1985–87

Telephone Operator connecting calls for subscribers

EDUCATION

Lingfield Comprehensive – 2 'O' Levels including English
TOPS Shorthand/Typing Government re-training
course   1987–88

INTERESTS

Playing the piano, creative cooking, car maintenance

Case study 6 is a good example of a winning CV which incorporates all of the elements outlined on pages 56–57 *except* element nine – personal. Date of birth and marital status are not given. You do have the prerogative of leaving this information out – after all it is *your* CV. There seems to be no apparent reason for Elizabeth to withhold this information. From the other dates it is not difficult to assess that she is over the age of 25 and below the age of 30, unless there was a long period of unemployment after leaving school. She may see such information as a potential hazard which could stop her from getting an interview if it was divulged during Application. In practice the omission did not stop her from getting interviews – *but it might have done if the remainder of the CV had not been so impressive.* As it is it does help to make the CV a *provocative* document and leaves much to discuss at an interview.

The profile is very forceful. She lays her cards on the table and states her objective. There is no way that this applicant is going backwards in her career. It is evident that she has *drive*. She started out as a telephone operator, showed *initiative* and made some financial sacrifice by undertaking a TOPS course and from then on worked her way up. There is *evidence* that she is an *achiever* and that others recognize the abilities/qualities that she has, eg ' . . . within 5 weeks promoted to Supervisor', ' . . . resolving word processing/printing problems of 5 other secretaries'. Elizabeth is not highly-qualified but no matter – this only serves to make her subsequent success more impressive.

CASE STUDY 7

MICHAEL BLAKE

The Old School House
Great Middleton
Nr Banstead
Berks. RD16 6AD   Home: 01855 476872

An effective and successful NATIONAL ACCOUNTS MANAGER with specialist knowledge of the licensed and grocery trades.

Key skills include:

* Self motivated and disciplined in the management of a trade sector and in the planning and organization of positive sales presentations.
* Achieving sales and marketing objectives by well planned personal effort.
* The creation of innovative and imaginative promotional activity.
* Responding early to deadlines. Working effectively under pressure.
* Implementing company policies to achieve an agreed marketing mix.
* Forecasting and budgetary control by brand within defined market sectors.
* Practical knowledge of stock and order and merchandising techniques.
* A clear concise communicator with verbal, written and reporting skills.
* Able to relate positively to clients and company personnel.

CAREER

DLC DISTILLERIES Ltd   1980–present

National Sales Manager – 1985–present

Developing own label brands within the major national grocery chains. Selling and promoting a mixed range of wines and spirits to all licensed trades outlets. Planning and organizing new product launches. Maximizing sales to existing customers. Opening and developing new outlets (30+ within a 9 month period). Liaising with wine producers to improve market penetration.

Area Manager   – 1980–85

Reporting directly to Managing Director for the sales and promotion of the spirits range within South East England. Achieving trade sector sales and marketing objectives through grocery chains; W/S and C&C; promotions including joint promotions with 'blue chip' companies. Management of sector includes forecasting and budgetry control by brand. Planning and organization of day to day operation.

BARRINGTONS BREWERS Ltd   1978–80

Sales Representative
The achievement of sales and marketing objectives in selling and promoting Barrington's brands to pubs and clubs.

THOMPSON PERROT Ltd   1975–78

Salesman
Selling to wholesale and retail chemists in South East. Consistently in top 5 of 30 sales force.

FOREST BANK Plc   1973–75

Accounts Department Supervisor
General Banking Duties: training, motivation and control of 10 staff.

EDUCATION AND TRAINING

Fenton Abbey School, Dorset: 7 'O' Levels, 3 'A' Levels
Full Tack Sales Training Course (1975)

PERSONAL

Date of Birth: 17.8.54   Married: 3 children

INTERESTS

Antique Restoration, Traditional Jazz (performing), most sports (watching)

Case study 7 really gives too much information, particularly in the first two thirds of the CV. Nine key skills is about three or four too many. The more 'key' skills you have the less effective they all appear. Despite making a brave attempt he hasn't quite mastered the art of condensing the information into concise 'telex' form. The continuous narrative is still there, largely due to the repetitive use of the word 'and' (see first skill description), which can usefully be dispensed with by using an oblique (/).

Michael may have forgotten that there is always the fall back position of using the accompanying letter to provide further information. It doesn't *all* have to go on the CV. He has completed a full Tack Sales Training Course yet this is (albeit logically) tucked away under 'EDUCATION AND TRAINING'. Such a highly respected and sought-after course deserves to be given greater prominence. This can be achieved by inserting it under the 'key skills' heading. To see how some judicious editing can improve a CV see the following condensed version:

MICHAEL BLAKE

The Old School House
Great Middleton
Nr Banstead
Berks. RD16 6AD   Home: 01855 476872

An effective and successful NATIONAL ACCOUNTS MAN-
AGER with specialist knowledge of the licensed and grocery
trades.

Key skills and achievements:

* Creating innovative/imaginative sales promotions.
* Full Tack Sales Training Course.
* Forecasting/budgetry control by brand within defined
  market sectors.
* Implementing company policies to achieve agreed market-
  ing mix.
* Managing trade sectors. Planning/organizing successful
  sales presentations.

CAREER

DLC DISTILLERIES Ltd   1980–present

National Sales Manager 1985–present

- Developing own label brands within the major national
  grocery chains.
- Securing/developing 30+ new outlets within a 9 month
  period.
- Selling/promoting mixed product range to all licensed trade
  outlets.
- Maximizing sales to existing customers.

Area Manager   1980–85

- Reporting directly to MD for sales throughout SE England.
- Achieving sales/marketing objectives to diverse range of
  retail outlets.

- Arranging joint promotions with 'blue chip' companies.
- Developing knowledge of stock, order and merchandising techniques.

BARRINGTONS BREWERS Ltd   1978–80

Sales Representative

- Achieving sales/marketing objectives in selling & promoting company brands to pubs and clubs.

THOMPSON PERROT Ltd   1975–78

Salesman

- Selling to wholesale/retail chemists in SE. Consistently in top 5 of 30 sales force.

FOREST BANK Plc   1973–75

Accounts Department Supervisor

EDUCATION: Fenton Abbey School, Dorset – 7 'O' & 3 'A' Levels

PERSONAL: Date of Birth 17.8.54   Married 3 children

INTERESTS: Antique Restoration, Trad Jazz (performing), most sports (watching)

CASE STUDY 8

CURRICULUM VITAE

NAME: Clive Harold James Morton

Address: 84 Reynolds Way
                 London SW11

TELEPHONE: 0171 632597

DATE OF BIRTH: 1st April 1972   AGE: 24

NATIONALITY: British

HEALTH: EXCELLENT

STATUS: Single

EDUCATION:

1978–1985   Shadwell Road Junior School, Wellington,
                 Herts.

1985–1990   Filton College, Colthorpe, Hants.
                 7 GCSE's

1 'AO' Level	–	French	C
3 'A' Levels	–	English Lit.	D
		Political Studies	D
		History	E

1991–1993   Brampton Polytechnic

                 Higher National Diploma in Business Studies.
                 Subjects covered included:

                 Accountancy, Economics, Business Admin.,

                 Advertising, Marketing, Computing,
                 Business Organization and Mathematics.

                 Institute of Linguists – French Grade 1

VACATION EXPERIENCE:

Sep 1990–Dec 1990   J. D. WOODS & Co – Northampton
Assistant Foreman in a Timber Yard.

Jan 1991–Jul 1991   INTERSTATE TRAVEL Ltd – London
Holiday Courier

Jul 1991–Sep 1991   MEGSONS ELECTRICAL Co Ltd – Brampton
Despatch Clerk and warehouse duties.

Jul 1992–Oct 1992   GLI COMPUTERS Ltd – Paris

3 months business experience and gaining
working knowledge of the language.

CAREER:

Jan 1993–present   LAMBTON COSGROVE SECURITIES Ltd –
London

Settlements Clerk dealing with many aspects
of settlements and assisting in the organization
of new issues. Computer input and telexes.
Distributed stock notes and helped cashiers.

Current salary: £16000 per annum
+ BUPA
+ mortgage subsidy
+ non contributory
   pension.

INTERESTS: Golf, sailing.

Case study 8 is an 'empty taxi' of a CV. Clive lays out the facts but reading it leaves one with no impression at all about *who* he is and where he is coming from (let alone where he is going). The problem is not so much that he conveys a negative self-image but that he conveys no image at all – it just doesn't hang together. If this CV sells anything at all it is mediocrity and superfluity. Clive shows no awareness of the need to sell skills, achievements or personal attributes and his selling of qualifications highlights low grade 'A' levels at the expense of his HND.

Clearly he has a wide range of work experience which must have allowed him to develop a number of skills, but the reader is left with too much work to do. It is not the reader's job to make the link between experience and skills/achievements/attributes. In that crucial first sixty seconds the reader does not have time to say 'Ah, his job as assistant foreman in a timber yard must have entailed supervising; checking; loading; unloading; stacking; and despatch of goods. Safety probably came into it as well . . .' Too much is left to the reader's imagination.

To compound the error Clive also omits to defend himself against potential hazards, inviting the following conclusions by the reader:

'No common thread running through his work experience – a fledgling job hopper perhaps?'

'We can match the salary but can't give a mortgage subsidy – he wouldn't be interested.'

'23 years old – too young.'

'Golf *and* sailing? – too time-consuming, we'll never see him.'

' "dealing with", "many aspects", "helped cashiers" – too vague, this doesn't really tell me anything.'

According to his CV Clive is still in work ('Jan 1993–present'), so why does he slip into writing in the past tense? 'Distributed stock notes and helped cashiers' could lead to confusion – if you are still in work don't give the impression that you might not be.

5 For school/college leavers

The techniques of writing a winning CV and accompanying letter differ little according to whether one is an experienced 'middle manager' or seeking a first job on leaving school. This separate section is for those of you who may have difficulty in identifying what you are selling and knowing how to present a good written case. In addition there are hazards to overcome which are peculiar to those seeking a first job. We strongly advise school and college leavers to read *all* of this book, not just this special section.

You will already have read that it is important to identify what you are selling and then sell it on paper through means of a CV and accompanying letter. We will now deal with each of these in turn:

WHAT ARE YOU SELLING?

- Experience?
- Achievements?
- Qualifications?

You will probably be selling all of these to a greater or lesser degree. School-leavers may feel that their GCSE or other qualifications are *all* they have to sell. This is rarely true: what you are selling depends entirely upon *what you have done and who you are.*

You may have been unaware of it but your CV really started

to take shape in your seventh year of school life (previously first form secondary). From then on what you did, both inside and outside school, was relevant to your future employer. The 'things we do' allow other people to make judgments on the type of person we are. It is on this basis that they will choose (or decline) to employ us.

'I can't get a job because I lack experience. I can't get experience because no one will give me a job.'

This is the age-old 'Catch 22' problem which haunts school-leavers but which so often is no more than an excuse for inertia. Of course lack of experience can, for some employers, be a barrier against employing school-leavers, particularly if they do not have the time (which is money) to train people, but from now on – forget it. Your task is to educate prospective employers to realize that you have more important things to sell.

We have already seen that experience *in itself* is not the all-important factor. *Skills*, *achievements* and the *evidence* for employers to identify *potential* all come out of experience. The good thing about potential is that you can sell it up until the age of about twenty-seven. After that the emphasis changes, because from then on you really have to begin selling achievements.

You must now start marshalling the facts and identifying what will go on your winning CV. The starting point is to look at your experience ('What I have done'). If your school has been helping you to keep a 'Record of Achievement' this will assist you. If not then you must go back to your seventh year of education (age eleven) and, working forwards, list the things you *did*. It is perhaps only now that your teachers' exhortations for you to 'join in and *do* something' become understandable!

If you have participated fully and are a 'doer' you may be able to develop something along the following lines:

- Youth club member (aerobics, weightlifting, archery)
- School debating team (County runners up)
- Scouting/Guides
- CCF (Combined Cadet Force)

89

- Drama club
- School prize winner (Essay)
- Prefect
- House Captain
- Duke of Edinburgh Award (Silver Medal)
- VSO/voluntary work in UK
- Set up and ran school club (computer, history, war games etc)
- Paper round
- Paid work during vacation
- Overseas travel (school trips, exchange visits)
- School orchestra
- Student representative on Board of Governors
- Represented school at athletics.

The list is not exhaustive. You will be very unlikely to have done all of the things listed and may have done other things not mentioned.

Now, the real question is 'so what?' What is the relevance of any of this to employers? They are all things you have done and are therefore 'experiences'. More importantly, they are experiences which allowed you to develop *skills, transferable skills* and *personal attributes*. Some of them can also be described as direct *achievements*. Your task now is to identify and describe what these experiences gave you. Consider the following list of personal attributes:

1 A good organizer
2 Able to work unsupervised
3 Flexible and receptive to new situations
4 Effective under pressure
5 Able to communicate with people at all levels
6 Dependable team member
7 Reliable and punctual
8 Self-motivated
9 Confident and concise communicator
10 Strong personality
11 Able to maintain a high standard of work
12 Excellent attendance record
13 Ability to demonstrate initiative
14 Conscientious
15 Tolerant

16 Good sense of humour
17 Good team leader
18 Ability to maintain accuracy under pressure
19 Organized and logical thinker
20 Able to set and achieve personal goals
21 Computer-literate and numerate
22 Excellent telephone manner
23 Sound administration skills
24 Able to supervise others effectively
25 Persuasive
26 Versatile
27 Possess common sense
28 Can solve problems and resolve queries
29 Can work to tight timetables and deadlines
30 Determined
31 Ability to delegate
32 Innovative and imaginative

Again, this is only a selection. Your task now is to undertake a matching exercise, ie match the appropriate *attribute(s)* to the *experience*.

Exercise

From your list of 'experiences' take each one in turn and go through the list of 'attributes' on pages 90–91. Write down the number of each attribute which you feel is applicable to the experience.

EXAMPLE:

- 'Paper round' 2, 7, 8, 12, 14, 29.

As you complete the exercise for each 'experience' you will probably find that certain 'attributes' recur. This is good news because each recurrence is further evidence that you do indeed possess such an attribute. The more frequently an attribute recurs the more confident you should feel about including such an attribute on your CV.

To employers, some experiences are self-evident in terms of the 'type of person you are'. They therefore speak for themselves. For example, if you *have* been awarded the Duke of Edinburgh's Silver Medal then it may not be necessary for you to say any more than that on your CV (although you can if you wish). Other experiences *and their relevance* are not so obvious to employers. This is where you have to educate them by establishing the *link* between an experience and its attributes. For example, to a layman 'archery' consists of little more than firing arrows at a target. Those who know about archery understand that there is rather more to it than that: it is a very character-building pastime and develops a wide range of attributes, ie:

- 'Archery' 4, 6, 8, 11, 18, 20, 27, 30

By completing this exercise you are making the link between what you have done (experience) and what it has given you as a result (attribute(s)). You are also supplying yourself with the *evidence* to support the statements on your CV. It is not good enough to simply say 'I am self-disciplined' – any prospective employers worth their salt are going to say to you at the interview 'Prove it'. If you complete this exercise carefully, thoughtfully and objectively (get your friends and parents to help you) you will provide yourself with the evidence to back up your written statements.

Now turn back to page 55 (CV layout) and read pages 56–57 (Action Checklist). The layout of your CV can be virtually the same as this but there will be the following differences:

Profile

Give up to three lines to your profile, which is designed to give the reader a brief summary of who/what you are. It can say whatever you want it to say, but what you choose to say will of course depend upon your employment objective. The following are some examples of useful profiles:

'A reliable, hard-working school-leaver with previous vacation work experience now seeking first permanent employment opportunity.'

'A well-qualified school-leaver with office-related experience, typing and VDU skills.'

'An honours graduate (2:1) in Business Studies seeking trainee management position within manufacturing industry.'

'A personable, well-presented school-leaver seeking first employment opportunity in a sales related environment.'

'An articulate, presentable school-leaver with some language skills seeking career opportunity in tourism/leisure industry.'

Don't be bashful about describing yourself in such a way. No one else is going to blow your trumpet for you. You have something good to sell – tell people about it.

Key skills

Having completed the previous exercise you will have identified a number of 'attributes'. Now is the time to sort out those which are relevant from those which are less relevant. Again, what you select and reject will be dependent upon your objective. What you decide to eventually put on the CV will be a selection in which you believe an employer will be most interested. Do not use the heading 'Key skills' if they are not all identifiable as *skills*. For example, 'conscientious' is not a skill but an 'attribute'; 'excellent attendance' is neither a skill nor an attribute but an 'achievement'. See what combination you have and then choose an appropriate heading. Examples are: 'Key skills and achievements'; 'Main attributes'; 'Key achievements and attributes'.

Career

For those of you seeking your first job, 'Career' is inappropriate and pretentious as a heading. 'Work experience' or 'Vacation experience' is more suitable.

Dates

You may need to state more exact dates than more experienced job hunters, for example: 'Jul–Sep 93'.

Education

If you feel that your educational qualifications are your major selling point then do not hesitate to move them into a more prominent position eg, between elements five and six.

The following pages contain examples of winning CVs for school and college leavers. They are not necessarily perfect and are not there to be copied slavishly. They are to be used as a model to illustrate the points made in this section.

CASE STUDY 9

PAUL ARNOLD

57 St. Michaels Road
Coatbridge
Manchester
M10 1EL   01532 216710

An articulate, presentable school leaver with some language skills seeking career opportunity within tourism/leisure industry.

Main achievements/attributes:

* Presenting information clearly and concisely in written and verbal form.
* Confident and effective in dealing with the public.
* Achieving set goals and working on own initiative.
* Queens Scout.

WORK EXPERIENCE

CUMBRIA OUTWARD BOUND CENTRE   Jul 94–Present

Assistant Team Leader

– Supervising teams of 8 adults undertaking various activities.
– Timetable planning and administrative tasks.
– Ensuring safety precautions strictly adhered to.

BLACKPOOL TOURIST INFORMATION OFFICE   Jul 93–Sep 93

Information Officer

– Resolving queries from UK and foreign national tourists.
– Liaising with hotels, leisure centres and authorities.
– Training 2 Assistant Information Officers.

EDUCATION

Coatbridge Comprehensive   Sep 91–Jul 94
6 CSEs (French Grade 1)
Currently studying French at evening class

Date of Birth: 5.6.76   Single   Full Driving Licence

INTERESTS

All sports (school cricket captain), Drama Club

Paul Arnold has certainly *made the link* between what he has done and the attributes this has allowed him to develop. There is plenty of evidence on the CV to back up his written statements, eg:

'presentable'

The employer won't find out whether Paul is presentable until the interview of course but Paul would surely not have been given an 'up front' job in an office if he were not presentable. In addition a Queens Scout is unlikely to be untidy. The excellent presentation of his CV also leads one to logically conclude that he cares about presentation.

'Presenting information clearly and concisely'

Paul's CV and his work experience is evidence of this.

'Confident and effective in dealing with the public'

Paul's whole CV oozes confidence. He has leadership ability: Queens Scout, Assistant Team Leader, cricket captain.

'Achieving set goals and working on own initiative'

Paul is clearly a 'doer' – he already has a full driving licence.

Paul negotiates the hazards very well. Notice what he is *not* selling: because his academic achievements are not earth-shattering he avoids selling low-grade CSEs. He did not join Coatbridge Comprehensive until he was fifteen. Why did he change schools? Did this have a detrimental effect on his education? Where was he before that? These questions remain unanswered at the application stage and rightly so – no CV should be clogged up with irrelevancies. Paul has been *selective* about what he is selling.

CASE STUDY 10

Green Mary Charlotte

Date of Birth: 1 Mar 79
Marital Status: Single

'Sunnybank'
Codrington-on-Sea
Essex
CT4 8BJ

Provisional driving licence   Telephone: Codrington 299809

EDUCATION & QUALIFICATIONS

School	From	To	Exam	Subject/Grade	
Codrington High	90	95	'O'	English Language	C
				French	C
				+ 6 CSEs inc Maths (1); Art (2)	
				RSA Typewriting Stage 1	

Further Education

Overdale College of F.E.	95	96	1yr F/T Business Studies Course (BTEC).

WORK EXPERIENCE

From	To	Employer	Job responsibilities
Jul 95	Sep 95	P. Burnside & Co Heath Estate Knighton	Typist/General Clerical work Invoicing/Customer queries/ Switchboard duties

(holiday job)

94 Summer hols		Low & Low Solicitors Kings Square Codrington	General office work Making appointments

INTERESTS

Home: cooking, decorating, sewing
Social: dancing, pop concerts, Youth Club
Sports: tennis, cycling.

REFERENCES

Miss C Adams	Mr. F. Low
General Manager	Low & Low
P. Burnside & Co	Solicitors
Heath Estate	Kings Square
Knighton	Codrington
KN5 5JG	CT8 5KD

Mary Green's CV *could* be a winner but if she is competing against other candidates during Application there is very little here to indicate that she is any different from her competitors. This CV is *messy* and thus difficult to follow. The dates are all over the place and there is unnecessary repetition – about as much space is devoted to selling her employers as to selling herself.

Mary has not identified the skills, achievements and attributes which have arisen from her experiences. What is Mary selling? It is unclear.

She is obviously sociable (good range of interests), likes to keep busy (interests, work experience during holiday) and seems keen to improve herself (F. E. Study). But how *good* is she? She does herself an injustice by merely relating her experience (what she has done) as nothing more than a series of responsibilities. There is no 'profile' which tells the reader quickly who/what she is (it is not necessary to state an 'objective' within the profile). Perhaps, above all, Mary comes across as *ordinary* – which is not good enough for a winning CV.

It is generally inappropriate to give details of referees on the CV, and is a waste of good selling space. This information can be given at the interview or in the accompanying letter. If your referees are particularly impressive then certainly highlight this on the CV. Let's see how Mary might have done better:

MARY GREEN

'Sunnybank'
Codrington-on-Sea
Essex
CT4 8BJ   01682 299809

A reliable, hard working student with knowledge of business
theory and some practical work experience.

Key skills/attributes:

* Maintaining high standard of work under pressure
* Ability to work unsupervised
* Arranging appointments for senior staff
* Excellent telephone manner
* Collating/checking invoices and resolving customer queries

VACATION EXPERIENCE

P. Burnside & Co – Knighton   Jul–Sep 95

Business experience in manufacturing company:
– ensuring timely despatch of products to UK wide retailers
– checking receipt of incoming raw materials
– liaising with suppliers and customers

Low & Low Solicitors – Codrington Jun–Sep 94

Administrative experience in legal environment:
– managing appointments and organizing travel arrangements for 4 very busy staff
– assisting County and Crown Court officials

EDUCATION

Overdale College of F.E.	— BTEC Business	1995–96
Codrington High	Studies	
	3 'O' levels including	1990–95
	Maths & English	
	Language	
	5 CSEs	
	RSA Typing Stage 1	

PERSONAL

Date of birth: 1.3.79	Single	Provisional driving licence

INTERESTS

Youth Club, Tennis, Cooking, Cycling, Dancing

The second version is certainly easier to read and is much more of a selling document. Mary has obviously thought more deeply about what she has done and what type of person she is. She uses the right 'ing' words to describe her skills (see pages 12–19).

There is a very important change of emphasis of which female job hunters may wish to take note. What isn't Mary selling on this revised CV? She is not giving prominence to 'typing' or 'switchboard duties'. Notice how 'switchboard duties' on the first CV has become 'excellent telephone manner' on the revised version. Notice also how 'typist' has disappeared altogether from her Jul–Sep 95 holiday job and how 'RSA Typewriting Stage 1' has been relegated to the bottom of the CV. *This* Mary Green does not see herself as a typist/secretary/receptionist and doesn't want others to see her in those roles either. She is undertaking a Business Studies course so presumably is anxious not to fall into (or be pushed into) that traditional slot reserved for female school-leavers. (Of course, if Mary *does* want to be a typist/secretary/receptionist then she will reinstate the appropriate skills/attributes/achievements.)

The two Mary Greens we have seen are an example of how the CV is *your* sales literature. Decide where you want to be, what you need to sell to get you there, and don't sell things which are likely to take you somewhere else or nowhere at all.

THE APPLICATION FORM

School-leavers and graduates may not always have the opportunity to present *any* CV let alone a winning one. Many established organizations have standard forms for applicants to complete. What you put on the form provides them with the basis upon which to judge whether you are worth seeing. Although filling in application forms is quite a chore great care must be taken. The real problem presented by application forms is that they provide fewer opportunities for you to present information about yourself as *you* would like it to be presented. Nevertheless, the following guidelines will ensure that you do as good a selling job as you can and that you avoid the hazards peculiar to application forms.

Step one

Before rushing into completing the form and getting rid of it as quickly as possible, get it photocopied. You can do this quite cheaply in libraries, some post offices and many shops that sell stationery and office equipment. Put the original form somewhere safe and do all your preliminary work on the copy.

Step two

Study the form. Familiarize yourself with the contents. What do they ask and in what way? How much opportunity is there to do a good selling job? How do they ask you to complete the form? If there are instructions eg, 'black ink', 'typed', then do exactly as they say. If there are no instructions either type (more professional) or print using a black pen. Never use blue ink – they may wish to photocopy the form and blue doesn't provide a good copy.

Step three

Never leave blank spaces. If a particular section is irrelevant to your situation put 'N/A' for 'not applicable'. If you leave it blank, the reader might assume that you have forgotten it or missed it altogether (hazard – 'lacks attention to detail').

Step four

Do the easy bits first. Much of the information is purely factual and need not require a great deal of thought eg, 'address' 'date of birth' etc.

Step five

Details of work experience, whether full-time or vacation work, are always requested. Under 'duties' or 'responsibilities' use the 'ing' skill description words (see pages 12–19).

EXAMPLE:

EMPLOYER	FROM	TO	DUTIES	SALARY	REASON FOR LEAVING
P. Burnside & Co. Solicitors	Jul 95	Sep 95	Ensuring timely Despatch of products to UK wide retailers. Checking receipt of incoming raw materials.	£200pw	End vacation
			Liaising with suppliers and customers.		

Note: There is rarely enough room on application forms. Do not try to squeeze everything in. Keep the information as concise as you can but do not be afraid to 'go over the boundary'.

Step six

Completing the 'Salary' section should not be a problem if you are seeking a permanent position and your previous experience has been vacation work only. For someone moving from one permanent job to another this can be more tricky. What you put under 'previous salary' is frequently used by prospective employers as a basis for considering what they will pay you. Strictly speaking, your previous salary is no one else's business so you might wish to be circumspect about what you choose to put. If they ask 'what salary are you seeking?' put 'tbd' for 'to be discussed'. If the salary is negotiable the application form is not the place to give them an indication of where you might want to start negotiating from.

Step seven

'Reason for leaving' is unlikely to be a problem if a vacation job simply came to an end – 'end vacation' will suffice. If you are moving from one permanent job to another give a positive reason for doing so eg, 'to broaden career' which you will of course be achieving if it is the right job.

Step eight

The section of the form to which you must pay great attention is that which states: 'Give your reasons for applying for this position', or more mysteriously, 'Give any other information in support of your application.' On no account leave this blank: that virtually guarantees that your application will be taken no further. This section of the form is in effect the equivalent of your application letter. Give the reader reasons why he or she *must* see you.

Look at the employer's needs. What do they want the successful applicant to do for them? Can you do it? If so *tell them*. Concentrate on what skills/attributes you can *contribute* and avoid drawing attention to those things you have not got or cannot do. Be positive, confident and relevant.

Step nine

Enclose your winning CV with the application form for use at the interview if they so wish. (Naturally you would prefer to do so anyway.) Do not make it *part* of your application, ie never write on the application form 'see attached CV' – this is extremely irritating to employers.

Before sending the documents, take a photocopy of each for your own future reference. Remember, you may not get an interview for some weeks, in which case you will want a record of what you said on the form and in your CV to refresh your memory. The employer will have them in front of him or her – don't put yourself at a disadvantage. The copy will also be useful the next time you have to fill in an application form. Attach a *brief* covering letter (see example). This is both courteous and businesslike and will set you apart from many of your competitors. It is also an opportunity for you to ask for an interview.

Letter to accompany application form

15 Stoneleigh Park
Henly
Lincolnshire
HN5 9HG

R Patterson Esq
ABC Holdings Ltd
Henly Industrial Estate
HN5 4PH

15 August 1996

Dear Mr Patterson,

Management Trainee (ref: RDC/16)

Please find enclosed your application form completed as requested.

For your additional information I have enclosed a copy of my CV which will also show the relevance of my experience.

I very much look forward to being called for an interview for this position and I can be contacted on 01936 451824.

Yours sincerely,

Mary Green

Mary Green

THE ADVERTISED VACANCY – ACCOMPANYING LETTER

As a school leaver or graduate you will not have the depth of experience or maturity to write such a forceful letter as Michael Evans (see page 127). But neither should you fall into the trap of writing a letter which is *weak, lacking in confidence, full of humility* and *apologetic*. You are not going 'cap in hand' begging for a job. Try to be confident without being 'cocky'. Whether you have qualifications or not be *proud* of who you are and what you can give to employers. You may have 'failed' your examinations but dismiss any thoughts of being *a* failure.

Projecting the right 'self-image' is very difficult if you feel that you do not have much to offer. But if your letter is *enthusiastic* it will be well received. Enthusiasm is infectious – if you have it they will catch it. To show how the *wrong* self-image can so easily project itself in an application letter, look at the following examples, which unfortunately are typical of those received by employers from school leavers.

'I hope that you will consider that my application is appropriate. I am free to come for an interview at any time.'

Of course your application is appropriate: a closing statement like that will only make the reader *doubt* the appropriateness of your application. The impression is that *you* are not entirely convinced it is appropriate. Why are you free to come for an interview at any time? Don't you have anything else to do? Although you are only trying to be accommodating it gives the impression that you are sitting around doing nothing.

'I hope that you will view my application with favour.'

Stop grovelling. If you must bow and scrape wait until *after* you have got the job. Do not confuse courtesy with servility.

'I hope that my qualifications and experience (if as yet somewhat limited) may merit your consideration.'

Never apologize for lack of experience, particularly if your competitors are likely to be fellow school-leavers or graduates. If they are looking to recruit 'first jobbers' they know already that you will not have much experience. Concentrate on what you *have* and not on what you lack.

Take a look at the following example of an advertisement:

TRAINEE SALES ASSISTANT

We have a vacancy in our Greychurch office for a Trainee Sales Assistant to learn all aspects of Estate Agency work. Applicants will ideally be presentable school leavers with preferably 2 'A' levels. Previous experience is not necessary as full training will be given.

Apply in writing to: The Managing Partner, Duttons Estate Agents, 10 Greychurch Road, Nottingham, NT4 6JD

Because the advertisement is not too specific it is likely to attract a large number of applicants, depending of course on the type of catchment area and the prevailing employment situation. It is reasonable to expect that no more than half a dozen of those applicants will be interviewed. The six who get an interview will be those who appear to be the most promising prospects on paper. Remember, that those *not* selected for interview may in reality have been equally promising – they simply failed to give the impression that they were.

What will the 'Managing Partner' be looking for?

- Evidence of presentability. Poorly-presented applications will be rejected even before they are read. Even an applicant who satisfies all of the other requirements will be knocked out of the game because of this.
- Qualifications. Lack of two 'A' levels need not on its own rule anyone out. The advertisement does only say 'preferably', but if the number of applicants is very high they may use this as their criteria for weeding out.
- Experience. Not really. But an applicant who does have some related experience may have an edge, not because of the experi-

ence itself but because it will reassure the employer that such an applicant actually *likes* that type of work.

- Enthusiasm. Any letters giving the impression that the writer just wants a job will be given short shrift. This employer at least will be investing time (ie money) in teaching the skills. Therefore the applicants really should sound enthusiastic about learning them.

- An understanding of what the job entails. Applicants would not be expected to have a great depth of knowledge but an indication that they saw it as more than just an office job would be encouraging.

The following is an example of what a 'winning' letter of application for this vacancy might look like.

10 Charles Street,
Greychurch,
Nottingham,
1 NT3 5BF

Mrs. P. Smith, 2
Managing Partner,
Duttons Estate Agency,
10 Greychurch Road,
Nottingham,
NT4 6JD

6 September 1996

Dear Mrs Smith,

Trainee Sales Assistant 3

Your advertisement 4 for the above position has interested me very much and I have pleasure 5 in enclosing my CV.

You will see 6 that I left school in July this year and since then have been working at ABC Ltd. They have asked me to stay on longer than intended and this I am pleased 5 to do. 7 But I am very keen 5 to begin a career with a leading 8 Estate Agency, hence my application.

During my vacation last year I had a job with the Housing Department. 9 This gave me useful experience and I 5

110

enjoyed helping people with their housing problems and showing them alternative accommodation. Because I seem to have a
flair 10 for this type of work the position of Trainee Sales
Assistant is exactly 11 what I am seeking.

I am presentable 12 and able to deal effectively 13 with people
and paperwork. For the above reasons I would welcome 5 the
opportunity of discussing the possibilities at an interview. 14
I can be contacted during the evening on Greychurch (01723)
765124 15

Yours sincerely,

Elizabeth James

Elizabeth James

Critique of Elizabeth James' letter

1 Remembered the post code – often neglected.

2 Has had the initiative and taken the trouble to find out a
   name – a phone call is all it takes.

3 This makes it immediately clear what the letter is about.

4 Declines to open with that dreary 'I' word which is so
   commonplace in application letters.

5 'Pleasure', 'pleased', 'keen', 'enjoyed', 'welcome' – these are
   all nice words to read: they exude enthusiasm, optimism
   and positive thinking.

6 'You *will* see' – positive and confident.

7 She must be a good worker if they want her to stay on.

8 Flattery is never wasted, provided you don't overdo it.

9 A previous job with the housing department is not ideally

relevant experience but she does go on to explain that some of the skills are appropriate.

10 Tells the reader in no uncertain terms that she has the ability to get results in this field.

11 Shows that she *knows* what she wants.

12 This was asked for in the advertisement. The presentation of the application is some supporting evidence of this.

13 Doesn't just make the point that she 'enjoys' dealing with people and paperwork – she is good at it.

14 Asks for the interview.

15 Gives her whole telephone number.

THE SPECULATIVE LETTER

For school-leavers and graduates wanting to find work near home the 'speculative approach' is essential. In June/July every year thousands of 'first jobbers' are launched into the job market. Although the numbers are declining the situation is still one of too many applicants competing for too few jobs. To stand a realistic chance of getting the *right* job at the *right* time and in the *right* place you really must take steps to eliminate your competitors by attacking the unadvertised job market.

Adopting the Action Plan below will enable you to make your approach in the right way, ie effectively.

Action plan

1 Define your geographical travel-to-work area. How far is it realistic for you to travel each day? Take into account such things as availability of public transport and *cost*. If you decide that 20 miles is a reasonable limit then there is little point in applying for jobs outside that radius. Your prospective

employers must lie within that radius. All you now have to do is find them!

2 Do your homework. Who are the key employers within your travel-to-work area? Make a list in Column 1 of the 'Target employer' sheet (page 115). Use the *Yellow Pages*. Your library is also a vital source of information: the librarian will provide you with reference books which will tell you not only the major employing organizations but give further information on them which will prove useful.

3 Study your local newspaper carefully. Your library or the newspaper itself may keep back copies which you can consult. Current and old job advertisements can be a very fruitful source of information. Look beyond the actual jobs advertised – employers might have *other* needs which you could satisfy but which they are not yet advertising. Read the whole of the newspaper. What business news is there? Which employers are advertising either themselves or their products? Who is applying for planning permission?

4 Once you have a 'hit list' of employers to whom you think it worth writing *find out something about them*. One use for this information will be in providing you with the opening to your letter, eg:

> 'Your company appears to be expanding in this area and I am interested to learn that you have received planning permission for a new office extension. For this reason it occurs to me that you may be seeking to supplement your number of office staff.'

You are really looking for signs of *movement* within an organization. Movement can be identified by observing the signals which indicate that the company is doing well eg,

> taking over new premises; relocating; advertising themselves or their products/services; taking over other organizations; moving into other activities; press releases on performance/intentions.

Having identified the signal which indicates movement write

113

it down in Column 2 ('Job lead') of the Target employer sheet.

5 Decide *who* to write to in the target organization. Although you are 'only' a school leaver/graduate, do not shrink from writing to the person at the top. Such people are often more approachable than you might think. They have not got where *they* are by beng reticent and have discovered for themselves that going straight to the decision-maker gets results. Write the name of your 'target executive' in Column 3 of the Target employer sheet. *Do not send your letter until all three columns are complete.*

For school/college leavers

Target employer sheet		
1 Name & address	2 Job lead	3 Target executive

In the following example, all 3 columns have been completed and a winning letter can now be constructed:

Target employer		
1 Name & address	2 Job lead	3 Target executive
R. J. Wilson & Co Welstead Business Park	Won Queens award to industry – Welstead Telegraph 15/5/96	Mr. R. J. Wilson

How to Write a Winning C.V.

The following is an example of a speculative letter to a prospective employer.

16 Copybush Road
Welstead
Yorkshire
WS9 4CF

R.J. Wilson Esq.,
Managing Director
R.J. Wilson & Co Ltd,
Welstead Business Park
Welstead
Yorkshire
WS9 3CJ

27ª May 1996

Dear Mr Wilson

Recent publicity indicated that through winning the Queens Award to Industry you are achieving orders from within the UK and overseas. For this reason I am writing to enquire whether you can use the extra help to cope with the demand.

In June, I will be leaving Welstead Comprehensive and am now seeking my first permanent job opportunity. You will see from my CV that I can offer a number of qualities you might find useful. Although I am perfectly capable of doing office work I am not afraid to "get my hands dirty" and would consider any opening to start with. Joining a successful company is my immediate objective and I am certain that I have the ability to progress in time.

Should you feel that I might be able to contribute to your continued success then I would be pleased to discuss the possibilities with you. I can be contacted by letter or in the evening on 01832 493420.

Yours sincerely

D. James

Critique of David James' letter

This would be a suitably winning letter from someone with no great qualifications and very limited experience. His CV would probably stress personal qualities rather than direct skills or achievements (he certainly possesses initiative). David is being completely 'open' about what *he* wants. He is giving the employer a great deal of leeway in terms of how he might be used – clerical worker, stores assistant, trainee fork lift truck driver, packer, etc. He is, quite rightly, not guessing at what the employer's needs might be – if you guess and get it wrong they may not think of offering anything else. What *is* interesting, and worth learning from, is the cumulative effect of the *words* David uses: winning, achieving, opportunity, capable, successful, objective, ability, progress, contribute. These are all words which send the right signals to the reader – what you say must reflect the type of person you are.

Notice that this particular letter is handwritten. This is an option open to you, even though you might have access to a typewriter and typing *is* more businesslike. A *neatly* handwritten letter on plain white A4 paper can nicely complement a typed CV.

Although David successfully avoids beginning with the word 'I' he subsequently makes up for this by using it *ten* times. This is not something to become obsessed about and you may find it desperately difficult to avoid, but do at least try to keep it under control.

The letter is *enthusiastic, confident,* and projects a *good self image* without going over the top.

The following is an example of how *not* to write a speculative letter:

117

Dear Mr. Harris,

Will you please consider me for a suitable vacancy within your organisation.

I am 18 years old and will be finishing a 2 yrs Business Studies (BTEC) National Diploma Course this June. During the course, I have been able to do part-time work, weekends and holidays, working for an Estate Agent — however, I do not wish to pursue that type of work for my career.

Working for your company appeals to me because you have a good reputation for giving young people the chance to prove themselves, also, I know several of your employees.

I enclose my CV and meanwhile would be grateful if you would grant me an interview.

Yours sincerely,

Critique

As speculative letters go it could have been much worse than this – trouble has at least been taken to write to a name. But great opportunities have been missed:

- Neither the opening nor the closing paragraphs are confident and enthusiastic. In fact, they are somewhat ingratiating and servile. In the final paragraph one can almost visualise the applicant (supplicant?) genuflecting while retreating backwards from the chamber.
- 'I am 18 years old' – there appears to be no real reason for highlighting this. Date of birth will be on the CV.
- Not enough is made of working for an estate agent. The writer is finishing (why not 'successfully completing'?) a Business Studies course and is presumably seeking to make use of what has been learnt. As an estate agency is a business there must be some relevance but the link is not made. The negative is accentuated rather than the positive – 'I do not wish to pursue that type of work' – the writer appears to see no benefits at all in the work experience he has had.
- The emphasis is on what the company can *give* ('young people the chance to prove themselves') rather than on what *he* can contribute. Chances sometimes have to be *made* rather than given. The employer is very unlikely to be influenced by the fact that the writer knows several employees.
- By saying 'I enclose my CV' in the final paragraph it comes across almost as an afterthought – as if the writer judges it as being of no great significance.

Overall the letter has not been thought through. It lacks discipline and the writer has clearly not stopped to consider how the reader might react to certain statements.

6 Completing the sales literature

Having constructed a winning CV it is now necessary to make an obvious, yet sadly neglected, point: *the CV never travels alone.* Unless you are handing it to a personal contact it will always be accompanied by a letter, the importance of which is disregarded by most applicants in the mistaken belief that the CV will do all the work for them. When making a formal application the CV *in itself* is unlikely to yield an interview. It is the combination of CV and accompanying application letter which does this. It is the failure to understand the relationship between the two which leads to poor applications – despite a winning CV.

The CV represents 50 per cent of your sales literature. The accompanying letter *complements* the CV and represents the other 50 per cent. The letter *individualizes* each application and *tailors* the application to a specific job. Giving the letter equal importance in effect allows you to have a general purpose CV because anything in your past which may be particularly relevant to a specific job, and which does not stand out in the CV, can be emphasized in the letter. This is why it is, or should be, misleading when we look at a CV in isolation – we are only reading half of the story.

The accompanying letter also *personalizes* the CV. It can 'flesh out' the bare bones and give an altogether more human aspect to the application. It can do this by displaying character and personality attributes such as enthusiasm, initiative, positive thinking and (carefully) humour.

CASE STUDY A

Just as letters can display personality/character attributes they can also, and frequently do, act as an advertisement for character *defects*. Perhaps the most common criticism to be levelled at application letters is that they are too self-effacing, even subservient, and often project an extremely poor *self image*. This is hardly surprising: since many job hunters are seeking work from a position of unemployment or impending redundancy, the self image is unlikely to be good. How we feel about ourselves is reflected in how we act and in what we say. To show how this and other factors can work against us we will look at Case study A. Read the following advertisement.

GENERAL MANAGER
(Manufacturing)
LIGHT ELECTRO-MECH. ASSEMBLY

The company produces a range of small units for use in a wide variety of manufacturing industries. Recent years have seen changes which have created one of the most efficient factories in the UK. The next step is to recruit a first-rate General Manager to control the production, design and engineering functions.

The ideal candidate should be in the age range 35–45 and be an engineering graduate with several years experience at a senior level in production management. This must have been within a light electro-mechanical assembly operation using modern systems to control well laid out production lines. The successful applicant must be a good administrator and experienced at handling industrial relations. We are particularly seeking applicants who are enthusiastic, progressive and have initiative.

Salary will be £35,000, a car is provided and re-location costs to Glasgow will be met if necessary.

Please send application letters and CVs to:

> The Personnel Director,
> XYZ Company,
> 20 Albert Square.
> Glasgow. G2 5PE

As advertisements go it is better than average. The employer begins by giving some background to the vacancy and proceeds to give a 'shopping list' of needs. It is quite likely that the employer would be willing to compromise on the age and qualification requirement provided the applicant has those requirements preceded by the word 'must'. There are indicators such as 'ideally', 'preferred' and 'likely' which tell us those factors on which they might be prepared to negotiate.

Mike Evans is going to apply for this job. He is aged 50, has no degree and is still working although due to be made redundant. He is deserving of an interview because he could do the job well and has many of the skills the employer is seeking. Unfortunately, the employer is not aware of this and Mike has chosen to highlight other things in his letter on the following page; things which will make the reader say 'no thank you'.

Mike's letter is typical of those received by employers every day. In fact, although it contains many of the cardinal errors, it is still better than many applicants' letters. He will not get an interview because he has *failed to overcome the hazards*. In Part 2 we discussed ten of the major hazards to be overcome when constructing a CV. Letter-writing is also hazardous but the hazards are not necessarily the same. The cardinal 'don'ts' specifically associated with letter writing are:

1 Unless specifically asked to do so never hand write your letter. Job hunting is business and business correspondence is *typed*. If you cannot type and do not possess a typewriter then buy one and teach yourself. It is an essential tool for the job hunter, it looks more professional and you will be learning a useful new skill. Regrettably, the art of good handwriting is dying and few of us have writing which is attractive – but job application letters are not the place to practise. At the rate at which you should be applying for jobs there simply will not be time to handwrite applications.

2 Type on white A4 paper. On no account use the proprietary brands we might use for social correspondence. All businesses use A4 paper so you will get off to a bad start by sending correspondence which doesn't fit their filing sys-

Completing the sales literature

64 Havant Drive,
Shedfield,
Edinburgh.

The Personnel Director,
XYZ Company,
20 Albert Square,
Glasgow G2 5PE

1st April 1990

Dear Sir,

I am interested in your advertisement in the Daily Telegraph and wish to apply.

I have spent a lifetime in manufacturing and have for the past 6 years been the Senior Production Manager in a light engineering environment which utilised computer controlled production techniques. I have now been made redundant because of the economic recession.

I am very interested in this position because it would give me the opportunity to utilise my experience and, as General Manager, give me more responsibility. Although I am over the age limit for this position I still feel that I can make a useful contribution to your organisation. I enclose my CV and hope to hear from you in the near future.

Yours faithfully,

M Evans.

M. E. EVANS

tems. If you are in doubt about how you should present yourself on paper then ring up and ask the employer.

3 Before writing your letter of application ring up the appropriate department (in this case personnel), ask if there is a 'job specification' for the position and elicit the *name* and *initials* of the person you are going to write to. Few of your competitors will bother to do this – it is just one very important means of ensuring that your application stands out from the other 99. If you were the Personnel Director would you not be impressed and intrigued to receive a letter from an applicant who has had the *courtesy* and *taken the trouble* to find out your name?

To underline the importance of this one Personnel Director I know will only consider interviewing applicants who have not chauvenistically assumed that she had to be a man to hold down a Personnel Director's job. Consequently any application letters (the majority) addressed to 'Dear Sir' were instantly consigned to the rejection pile, *regardless of their other merits*.

Competition in the job market is such that it is not unusual for employers to incorporate a little initiative test into the advertisement itself. Some advertisements request you to send applications in writing to, for example, 'Joan Smith'. Now when you write to 'Joan Smith' how do you address her? 'Dear Madam'? (too formal), 'Dear Joan'? (Never!), 'Dear Mrs Smith'? (how do you know she is married?), 'Dear Miss Smith'? (How do you know she is single?). The *only* way to ensure that you have it right is simply to telephone and ask 'how does Joan Smith like to be addressed?' This in itself will not guarantee you an interview but you have cleared the first hurdle – which *may* have been deliberately put there. You have also made that first important contact which may give you a 'friend at Court'. The only excuse for not making the call is if you are given a box number to write to. Do not be suspicious of box numbers. There is often a good reason for using them: an employer may not wish competitors to know that they are recruiting, or the present post-holder to know that he or she is being replaced.

4 As with the address on the CV, include your postcode. Lack of attention to detail could cost you dear.

5 Avoid the repetitive use of the word 'I'. This is a common error and particularly noticeable when used at the beginning of a paragraph. With a little effort it is possible to eradicate it. It cannot be eliminated altogether but over-use does tend to make the letter too 'self' orientated.

6 You must make it immediately clear *which* position you are applying for. Remember that they may have advertised more than one position. If they give a reference number, quote it.

7 The first paragraph sets the tone of the letter so it is important to get off to a good, confident start. Mike Evans's letter fails in a number of respects. In the first paragraph he:

- Begins with the word 'I'.
- Doesn't specify the job.
- 'Wishes' to apply – never use this word. Employers don't want 'wishers'.
- Fails to convey *enthusiasm*.

8 Don't draw attention to weaknesses. Mike may understandably feel that 'spending a lifetime' in manufacturing is a good way of saying 'look how experienced I am'. Unfortunately the reader is more likely to interpret this as 'look how *old* you are'. As indicated on pages 27–28, be careful about selling experience through time.

9 If you are job hunting from a position of redundancy be very careful about how you get this across because it can have a negative effect upon the 'self-image' you are projecting. It is better not to mention it at all (let alone give excuses, such as blaming the economic recession, as Mike does). *Why* you are in the job market is irrelevant during Application – they can ask you this at the interview, which is by far the best place to discuss it. If you cannot resist mentioning redundancy, always remember that *jobs* are made redundant not *people*. If you go around saying '*I* have been made

redundant' you are personalizing the situation (which is incorrect) and encouraging readers who don't know any better to question your ability, or even integrity.

10 You must make it clear *what* you are selling and *how* you can fulfil the employer's needs. 'I am very interested . . . give me more responsibility' is too self-orientated. Mike is emphasizing *what they can do for him* rather than what *he* can contribute. Although the advertisement made it quite clear what the needs were, no attempt is made to match those needs. The letter conveys all the wrong signals.

11 Never give reasons why an employer *shouldn't* interview you. 'Although I am over the age limit' is a classic example of advertising one's Achilles Heel. If age really is a bone of contention, the employer will be quite able to work it out from the date of birth on the CV. As the song goes 'Accentuate the positive, eliminate the negative'. If you do this then the reader is that much more likely to 'latch on to the affirmative'.

12 Choose your words carefully. For a salary of £35,000 we could not criticise the employer for expecting more than just a 'useful contribution'. Mike writes: '– hope to hear from you –'. Never 'hope' – employers no more want 'hopers' then they do 'wishers'.

13 If you are still in work on no account give the impression that you might not be. Mike falls into this trap by implying that he is already out of work when in fact he is still on the payroll of his employer. Your *job* does not become redundant until the last day of termination of contract. Any redundancy notice you are under (normally ninety days) is the *optimum* time for you to seek work. It is easier to get another job while you still have one:

'The single consistent (employment) trend discernible is that people wanting to change their job while already employed are in a far, far better position than those no longer on some regular payroll.'
('Jobkey' New Opportunity Press/PER).

14 Given that the whole purpose of writing the letter is to get an interview, it might be a good idea to ask for one. Even saying, 'I look forward to hearing from you', is a weak ending and adds to that lack of enthusiasm which permeates Mike's letter. This is particularly damaging since enthusiasm was one of the qualities asked for in the advertisement.

Clearly, even if Mike has a winning CV (which is unlikely as losing CVs typically accompany losing letters) he has a lot of work to do to bring his letter up to scratch. The following is an example of how he should have written the letter.

42 Chesnut Drive,
Dewsbury,
Yorkshire,
YK4 6LP

Mrs P. Thomas,
Personnel Director,
XYZ Company,
20 Albert Square,
Glasgow.
G2 5PE

2 April 1996

Dear Mrs Thomas,

General Manager

Your advertisement for the above position has interested me very much and I now apply.

You will see from my CV that my career in manufacturing has progressed through jobs of increasing responsibility to the point where I am now a Senior Production Manager.

In my present position I am responsible for the production, design and engineering functions of a light engineering operation. My initial brief was to introduce a fully automated assembly operation into the Plant within five years. This I achieved ahead of schedule and the system in now running at 20 per cent cost savings per annum. This success is due in no small way to careful and continuing consultation with the 450-strong workforce through the Trade Unions, and using a unique incentive scheme I introduced and which has now been adopted throughout our other UK plants.

Having succeeded in my task and seen the operation through to completion I am now seeking to broaden my career. The position of General Manager with your company is exactly what I am seeking and I feel that my experience, enthusiasm and administrative skills could be used to good effect by XYZ Company.

I would be very pleased to attend an interview for this position and can be contacted by letter at the above address or during the evening on 01924 465321.

Yours sincerely,

Michael Evans

Michael Evans

It is hard to believe that the revised letter is from the same person who concocted the first one. Which Mr Evans would *you* interview? What makes the second letter much more likely to achieve an interview?

- He has included his postcode and taken the trouble to find out the name of the Personnel Director. Displays the initiative they specifically asked for.
- The letter is well-presented, nicely typed and contains no errors (no matter that it may have taken six attempts to get it right).
- Although he is over the age limit, has no degree and his present job is due to become redundant, Mike is not wearing his heart on his sleeve. He *knows* he can do this job and is saying so.
- Unlike many of his competitors for the job he is confident enough not to 'wish' or 'hope'.
- He has not fallen into the trap of expecting his CV to do all of the work for him. He is highlighting those aspects of his career which are *relevant* to this particular job. He will, of course, take the precaution of stapling his letter to the CV to prevent it from becoming detached.
- He is encouraging the reader to look at the CV: 'You will see . . .', '. . . I am now a Senior Production Manager.' This

forces the reader to glance at the CV to see who he is currently working for.

- He is not 'redundant' but *ambitious*: 'Seeking to broaden my career'.
- He is ensuring that his present job title (Senior Production Manager) does not give the wrong impression. He makes the point that he is responsible for production, design and engineering which was mentioned in the advertisement.
- He uses optimistic, positive words like 'achieve', 'success' and 'progress'. This all helps to present a positive self-image. We all like to employ successful, progressive achievers.
- He *quantifies* his achievements and responsibilities. This gives the reader a clearer idea of his capabilities.
- He makes it clear that he can not only meet his targets but *exceed* them. The reader is forced to conclude that here is a person who can *get results*.
- He is aware that a business exists to make a profit. He has the ideas to increase profit margins (20% cost savings).
- He has clearly *studied* the advertisement. He is not content to just say 'I am experienced at handling industrial relations'. He makes this point by giving a practical example.
- He has *intrigued* the reader. Can they afford *not* to find out more about that unique incentive scheme?
- There is no humility in the letter. Even though it may go against his natural inclination, he knows that if ever he is going to blow his own trumpet this is the time to do it. It is important not to overdo this for there are great rewards to be had from heaping praise on others and emphasizing the importance of teamwork, but this is used to best effect at the interview.
- He remembers to ask for the interview and ensures that his full telephone number follows it up. When the letter is being read, the reader's telephone is usually but a few tantalizing centimetres away – make them pick it up.
- There are just as many 'I' references as in the first letter but they are unobtrusive because they do not come at the beginning of sentences or paragraphs.

In this Case study we have seen two quite different responses to the same advertisement. They display quite different attitudes to the predicament, which are reflected in the *quality* of the respective letters.

The first shows an applicant already defeated. Because he saw himself as a failure he *was* a failure – he could only see his situation as it was and no further. He believed he was applying for a *job* and if he had any goal at all it was probably simply to write a letter – any letter.

The second shows an applicant with *vision*. He is not dwelling on the situation as it is but *as it is going to be in the future*. He is a success because he sees himself as a success. He understands that although his ultimate goal is to get the job offer his immediate objective is to get through to an interview. Take one step at a time.

When you have drafted a letter in response to an advertisement, check it for quality by ticking the appropriate box in the following Action checklist when the action has been taken.

Responding to an advertised vacancy – action checklist

- Typed. A4 good quality paper. No errors? ☐
- Asked for a job description? ☐
- Written to a name? ☐
- Specified clearly the job for which you are seeking interview? ☐
- Minimized use of the word 'I'? ☐
- No 'wishing' or 'hoping'? ☐
- Used positive words: 'achieve', 'success' 'contribute'? ☐
- Studied the advertisement – identified their needs? ☐
- Shown how you could meet those needs? ☐
- Conveyed enthusiasm. Good self image? ☐
- Quantified where appropriate? ☐
- Accentuated the positive. Eliminated the negative? ☐
- Shown that you can get results? ☐
- Intrigued the reader? ☐
- Paid attention to detail? ☐

- Asked for the interview? □
- Given your full telephone number:? □
- Attached your letter to the CV? □
- Is your letter the *best* example of the work you are capable of producing? □

CASE STUDY B

Given that only 25 per cent of job vacancies are advertised it really is essential that you devote much of your time and effort to exploring the *unadvertised* job market. To do this effectively requires a quite different approach. The *speculative letter* incorporates many of the techniques one would use when responding to a job advertisement, but because the potential hazards are somewhat different there must be some subtle changes of style and emphasis. There are two basic methods that can be adopted:

1 The 'Shotgun' or 'Blunderbuss' approach. A very unsophisticated method, generally lacking in direction and consisting largely of a massive output of letters fired off in random directions. Can be effective provided the output is great enough and your type of work is not too specialized.

2 The 'Sniper's' approach. With this more sophisticated method one well-aimed shot can get a good result. You target specific employers for whom you particularly want to work and who have given you reason to believe they have a vacancy. Your output of letters need not be so great but you do need to put more work into each one. A rewarding approach for those in fairly specialized fields of employment.

To see how both of these techniques might work in practice, let's look at the following approach. Pauline Anderson is a Customer Services Officer currently working for Countybank in London. Her job is due to become redundant and she is now interested in moving back to Cardiff:

10 Denmead Road,
Oxted Park,
London N14 4PQ.

M. Thompson Esq.,
Personnel Manager,
Moneybank plc,
Greystone Road,
Cardiff,
CF2 1FH

28 July 1996

Dear Mr. Thompson,

I am writing to ascertain whether or not there is a vacancy within your organization.

I enclose my CV which illustrates my experience to date.

The position I hope to obtain is that of Customer Services Officer in your mortgage department or even Customer Services Manager if you have a vacancy (I have experience of deputising for my Department Manager). My present job is due to become redundant at the end of next month and I am hoping to return to Cardiff which is my home town.

If you have a suitable vacancy I would be pleased to hear from you and of course come to Cardiff for an interview.

Yours faithfully,

Pauline Anderson

Pauline Anderson

Pauline has clearly chosen the 'Shotgun' approach! There are *some* good things about the letter and if Moneybank plc *do* have a current vacancy for a Customer Services Officer/Manager she may well achieve an interview. Using her letter as our guide we will look at the good and bad points, paying particular attention to why she might *not* get an interview:

1 The letter is well presented and trouble has been taken to write to a *name*. But is it the *right* name? Personnel Departments

will often be unaware that a vacancy has arisen within an organization. They are made aware when the time has come to *do something about it*, ie advertise or brief recruitment agencies. Your task is to reach the organization during that 'window' of time between when the need arises and when they get around to fulfilling that need. If you go straight to the personnel department, they are quite likely to respond by saying they have no vacancy – as far as they are aware this is probably true. Alternatively they might say that they have a vacancy and will be advertising next week. In this instance the window of time has closed and you will have competition for the job.

To avoid this you must identify, and write to, the key decision-maker for the function at which you are aiming. Line managers and Heads of Department are more likely to be aware of a vacancy before personnel departments are made aware.

Pauline complicates this issue by being *too specific* in terms of *what she wants*, ie 'Customer Services Officer in your mortgage department or even Customer Services Manager'. If she were simply seeking a Customer Services Officer's position then writing to the present Customer Services Manager would be the correct approach, but writing to the Customer Services Manager and asking for *his or her job* is unlikely to generate a reply let alone an interview. It is only human nature to resist recruiting someone who might pose a threat to one's own job security.

If in doubt about *who* to write to in an organization then go straight to the top. Travelling first class gets results and a speculative letter will get more attention if it is addressed to the Managing Director. It will almost certainly filter down through the system but the person whose desk it eventually lands on will be more inclined to do something positive about it.

2 Pauline makes the usual mistakes of tedious repetition of 'I' and use (twice) of the word 'hope'. There is something about the word 'hope' which doesn't sound very hopeful at all.

3 Avoid using the word 'vacancy' in a speculative letter. You

need to be more subtle if they haven't advertised. 'Position', or preferably 'opening', is more correct. The same goes for the word 'interview'. Remember that employers for the most part do not particularly *enjoy* going through the formal process of recruiting. The words 'vacancy' and 'interview' can ring all kinds of alarm bells for them which are based on previous experiences. You do not want to awaken such feelings. Asking for 'a meeting to discuss the possibilities' is less formal and certainly less threatening.

4 Although Pauline describes her present position in the right way, ie 'My present *job* is due to become redundant' there really is no need at all to explain *why* she is in the job market: this can be discussed at a meeting. She really ought to sound more confident and definite about her intention to return to Cardiff, eg 'I *will be* returning to Cardiff'.

5 She signs the letter 'Yours faithfully' which is incorrect when writing to a person by name. 'Yours sincerely' is correct.

6 The most significant error Pauline makes it getting the *emphasis* wrong. Mr Thompson will quickly conclude that the only reason she is writing to him is because she needs a job in Cardiff; there is no indication that she wants to work for Moneybank rather than any other organization, and no emphasis on what she can offer them. It stands to reason that a letter will generate much more interest if it tells the reader what is on offer and declines to express what the writer is looking to get out of it. The impression is that names and addresses have been plucked out of the Cardiff telephone directory and Moneybank is just one of many on the list. This in fact is the biggest drawback of the 'shotgun' approach.

To stand an improved chance of achieving a meeting, Pauline should try the more sophisticated 'Sniper's' approach, as follows:

10 Denmead Road,
Oxted Park,
London N14 4PQ.

C. Charles Esq.,
Managing Director,
Moneybank plc,
Greystone Road,
Cardiff,
CF2 1FH.

28 July 1996

Dear Mr. Charles,

Your Annual Report states that in the coming year you will be
expanding your home loans department and making mortgages
more readily available to customers. For this reason it occurs
to me that you may well have an opening for someone with
my skills and experience.

You will see from my CV that I can offer the following relevant
expertise:

- Interviewing customers, vetting loan applications and resolv-
  ing customer queries.
- Supervising and training of junior staff.
- Liaising with solicitors and other external organisations.

I will shortly be returning to my home town of Cardiff and am
seeking to broaden my career with a leading clearing bank such
as Moneybank plc. Should you feel that you can utilize my
skills I would be very pleased to come to Cardiff and discuss
the possibilities. I can be contacted by letter at the above address
or in the evening on 0171 456789

Yours sincerely,

Pauline Anderson

Pauline Anderson

Why is this letter more likely to achieve a result?

1 Right from the word 'go' Pauline is concentrating on *the*

employer and not on herself. Employers are always more interested in themselves than in you, so starting off with the word 'you' or 'your' will grab their attention.

2 Pauline displays *company knowledge*. Having done her homework she makes the point that she has done it. They are bound to be attracted by someone who has had the initiative to send for their Annual Report. This also makes it clear that the writer has not just plucked them out of the telephone directory.

3 The reader is encouraged to look at the CV by 'you will see', but to back this up Pauline emphasizes what she can *'offer'*.

4 Note that Pauline does not emphasize her current job title, nor does she stipulate what *she* wants. She does encourage the reader to believe that she can improve upon her present position. This is done by highlighting her supervisory and training experience and by indicating that she is interested in broadening her career. This of course also implies that she is ambitious or at least career-minded.

5 Indulging in a little flattery never goes amiss. We all like to feel that we work for one of the 'leading' companies in our field.

6 She doesn't ask the employer to carry out a formal 'interview' but requests a 'meeting'.

7 The letter is deliberately *brief*. This is even more essential with a speculative approach because you have very little to go on: the more you say the more probable it becomes that the employers will find something to put them off.

The benefits of a speculative approach

- In one bound you are eliminating your *competitors*. In effect you are playing 'Application' all on your own – a much more healthy state of affairs. Because there is no competition the reader will not be under pressure and will have more time to consider your letter.

- It is a way of reaching the employer before he or she has gone firm on the 'person profile' sought. In such circumstances employers are more amenable to making the job fit *you*. Once they have decided to advertise and made a decision on such things as age, qualifications and experience they can be harder to budge.
- You are displaying *initiative* and showing that you are a pro-active person. You are clearly not the type of person to sit around waiting for something to happen.
- Recruitment through the normal channels is time-consuming and hence costly for the employer. You are potentially saving him or her a lot of money.
- In Part 1 we established that in job hunting you are the seller and the employer is the buyer. With the speculative approach you are fulfilling the true function of a seller ie *advertising* that you have something for sale. In any other walk of life we do not expect *buyers* to advertise a need. Perhaps this is why so few employers do advertise.

Below is an 'Action Checklist'. When you have drafted a speculative letter check it for quality by ticking the appropriate box when the action has been taken:

The speculative approach – action checklist

- Found out something about them? 1 ☐
- Identified and written to the key decision-maker? 2 ☐
- Not used the words 'job' or 'vacancy'? 3 ☐
- Started letter with 'you' or 'your'? 4 ☐
- Emphasized what skills you can contribute? 5 ☐
- Not been too specific about *your* needs?? 6 ☐
- Introduced an element of intrigue? 7 ☐
- Conveyed enthusiasm and good self-image? 8 ☐
- Asked for a meeting? 9 ☐
- Given your full telephone number? 10 ☐
- Finished with 'Yours sincerely'? 11 ☐
- Been sufficiently brief? 12 ☐

CASE STUDY C

15 Sudbury Square,
Liverpool,
LP8 4JK

S. Potter Esq.,
Chief Representative Europe,
Pan Airways,
P.A. House,
Ruislip,
Middlesex,
MD1 IL0

15 August 1996

[2] Dear Mr. Potter,

[4] Your airline's reputation and success within the airline industry has very much impressed me. [1] With the launch of your Peking–London service beginning in December, and further routes planned, it has occurred to me that you [3] may well have an opening for someone with my marketing background (in the UK or overseas).

From the enclosed CV you will see that whilst with Sams Airways I have gained experience in the area of strategic marketing, which includes [5] designing [8] successful marketing plans and promotional strategies for new routes [7] (one of which was Peking); implementing advertising [5] campaigns, [5] evaluating joint ventures and [5] reviewing the effectiveness of past promotions on sales. [12]

[8] I am now seeking to broaden my experience within an airline such as yours, and would [8] welcome the prospect [6] of working in the more frontline areas such as product and sales management development. It is also likely that my skills could [5] contribute greatly to your plans for developing new routes.

Should you be interested in discussing the possibilities I would be ⑨ very pleased to come and see you. I am available during the day ⑩ on 01426 684321 or in the evenings on 01426 894377.

⑪ Yours sincerely,

Mark Clarke .

Mark Clarke

Mark's letter satisfies all of the requirements on the action checklist, so does this make it a 'winning' speculative letter? It probably goes as far as it can. Much will depend upon 'Mr Potter's' perception of it and whether there is a need which he believes Mr Clarke might be able to fill. It is certainly confident and forceful without going 'over the top'.

Failure to secure a meeting will not necessarily make it a 'losing letter'. You can't win 'em all. This illustrates the point that it would be foolish to rely on a 'one-off' speculative letter. If you want to get the right job quickly your output must be quite considerable.

Perhaps the real question is 'could *you* write such a letter?' Try to develop your own style while at the same time incorporating the main guidelines. Because it is not 'social' correspondence you are not supposed to feel particularly *comfortable* with it – it is a marketing document after all, and the 'Cringe Factor' (see page 60) applies as much to the letter as it does to the CV. But you *must* be able to back it up at the meeting – many applicants fail to secure job offers because although they can 'talk the talk' they can't 'walk the walk'.

Conclusion

In conducting an intensive job search campaign you will no doubt submit an occasional application for a position which is *not* suitable for you. An interview will not be forthcoming because they will *see* that you are unsuitable. This should not alarm you at all – even a winning CV cannot compensate for the fact that *they* won't always want what you are selling. But if you are consistently failing to achieve interviews for jobs that you know to be right then this is cause for concern.

A letter of rejection will typically state that 'We have received a large number of applications for this position and will be interviewing those who appear to be more suitably qualified . . . .'. You can interpret this more accurately as 'You failed to sell us other things which would have compensated for your lack of qualifications.' Another typical response would be along the lines of 'We will be interviewing more suitably experienced applicants.' Again, you can interpret this as 'We couldn't see the relevance of your experience'. If you know that your experience is relevant then they couldn't see it because you *failed* to *make* them see it. You may have felt that the relevance was so obvious that it didn't need selling – perhaps you were too blasé. Whatever the reason any failures are down to you and it is tme to review your sales literature.

Poor players of 'Application' don't get to play 'Interview' as often as they ought. Successful players achieve more interviews, not because they are more suitable for the job (although they may be), but because they understand the two most fundamental rules of the 'Application Game':

Conclusion

1 Selling your strengths maximizes the chances of achieving the interview.

2 Defending your weaknesses minimizes the risk of *not* getting the interview.

These two fundamental rules have formed the underlying basis of 'How to Write a Winning CV'. Playing a successful game is dependent upon not just knowing why applicants are selected but why they are sometimes *rejected*. All good salespeople know that the principles of selling and advertising are based upon both product strengths *and* product weaknesses. You are now in a stronger position to identify what you are selling and to counter any objections to that sale. By putting into practice the rules of the game you will diminish the element of chance. Don't be an 'Empty Taxi'.

Index

145

HOW TO NEGOTIATE YOUR SALARY

ALAN JONES

Many of us accept jobs or new positions at a salary level lower than we might have achieved if only we had tried to negotiate a better deal. The ability to bargain is not highly developed in the average job hunter, and there is a tendency to think that asking for more money might prejudice your chances of getting the job at all.

In How to Negotiate Your Salary Alan Jones demonstrates how mistaken this attitude is. He shows how to overcome the traditional reluctance to negotiate and how to get the very best package of salary and benefits when going for a new job or seeking a pay rise in your current situation.

Read this highly practical book and enter salary discussions fully prepared and confident of maximizing your earnings in such a way that both you and your employer are happy.

£7.99
ISBN 0-7126-5391-0